How to Write Successful Foundation Presentations

by Joseph Dermer

The Taft Group
12300 Twinbrook Parkway, Suite 520
Rockville, MD 20852

Contents

WRITING THE APPOINTMENT LETTER 7

APPEALS FOR GENERAL PURPOSE GRANTS 16

SPECIAL PROJECT PRESENTATIONS 28

WRITING THE BUILDING PROPOSAL 59

LETTERS OF RENEWAL 72

CONCLUSION 79

Foreword

It has been stated that the best way to write a foundation appeal is to have it signed by the niece of the foundation trustee to whom it is directed.

Let it be said that there is more than a grain of truth in this viewpoint. Personal relationships frequently do play a role in the process of securing a foundation grant. But so, indeed, does an awareness of how to approach a foundation, a knowledge of what to stress, a sense of logic and order, and a capacity to communicate effectively. That is what this manual is all about.

This manual was first published in 1970, went through several printings and is now being republished with a rather considerable number of changes. About 40% of the material is all new.

For example a number of readers wanted a greater variety in letters which would provide guidance in asking appointments with foundations. Hence this chapter has been considerably expanded.

Still other readers expressed a need for examples and commentaries on proposals requesting grants for buildings or for securing equipment. So a whole new section has been added covering just this subject.

Other sections of the manual—appeals for general purpose grants, special project proposals and letters requesting renewals—all have been revised and contain new material.

About the examples: they are authentic; which is to say that they were written not to serve as guides for anything, but, rather, to accomplish a specific purpose (e.g., get an appointment, a grant, or renewal of a grant). However, to preserve the anonymity of the organization concerned, we have introduced elements in each example, or withheld certain other elements, so as to make it impossible to identify the particular organization.

The examples you will read were successful in achieving their basic objective. You will, however, be making a considerable mistake if you attempt to use any part verbatim in your own work. Aside from a general familiarity that is resulting insofar as specific wording is concerned, it is likely that the wrench in shoving your agency into a pre-existing context of words will be evident.

Rather, pay particular attention to the commentary that accompanies the examples. The points they make are universal insofar as anything can be considered universal in the foundation world. They represent, also, a distillation of twenty years of experience in dealing with foundations and foundation officials.

Underlying this manual, and everything that appears in it, is a basic assumption. It is, simply, that the organization for which you seek foundation support deserves to receive such support, but may not have been effective in putting its best writing foot forward. If that is not the case, this handbook will not help you one whit. If it is, we believe you will be taking a significant step toward securing the kind of foundation support you want.

Good luck!

Writing The Appointment Letter

There is a process in the securing of a foundation grant, and the first step in that process usually is getting an appointment.

It is true, of course, that on occasion an application will reach the right foundation with the right request at the right time, and a grant will be forthcoming. But the instances in which this happens are, comparatively speaking, so rare that you are far better off seeking an appointment. This is true even if the foundation is not in your general area. (See letters C and D.) Obviously, though, if you are attempting what may be a kind of foraging expedition, it's a good idea to try to get appointments with a number of foundations. We are assuming, of course, that you have done your basic research and know that these foundations, at least in general, are interested in your organization's activities.

On the pages that follow are a number of appointment letters from a variety of organizations. All were successful in securing appointments. All have certain things in common. Let's look into that, first.

For one thing, they are brief—the longest is about half a type-written page. Beyond this, they stick to a single, simple point; they request a meeting for a particular purpose. If the purpose is to discuss a special project, only the essentials of the project are given. If a general purpose grant is sought, only the special circumstances justifying such a grant are given.

We emphasize the need to keep your appointment letter as lean as possible for a basic reason. The possibility exists that overabundant writing may submerge and ultimately drown the single purpose of the letter: securing an appointment. If the request to see the foundation official is part of a lengthy exposition, he may feel that he already has enough information to make his judgment without seeing the applicant. Thus, a decision will be reached on the basis of a "proposal" which is not really a proposal at all—just a letter which stands in grave need of dieting.

Incidentally, as you will note with certain of the examples that follow, it's perfectly all right to include a piece of literature—perhaps an Annual Report, which describes, generally, the work of your organization.

Now, let us turn directly to some actual letters. Letter A is from an organization concerned with interracial relationships. Letter B is from an international child service agency. Both letters concern special projects. Note how brief and to the point they are and yet how much information they communicate. Both letters mention the cost of the project; but the writers are careful not to indicate that they hope to secure the full amount from the particular foundation concerned. Depending on what happens at the actual meeting, this may or may not be the case.

LETTER A

Dear Mr. ....:

May I meet with you to discuss an important new project which (Name of Agency) hopes to undertake.

Briefly, it is this: With the construction of the Verrazano Bridge, the United States Census Bureau projects a nearly 100 per cent increase in Staten Island's Negro population from its present level of 16,000 to 30,000 by 19—. We realize that this large influx of Negro families and individuals, together, indeed, with many other newcomers, may affect community relationships in Staten Island, and we should like to act now to develop a harmonious and positive situation within the community.

Specifically, we wish to undertake, as soon as possible, a two-year pilot community program encompassing housing, economic development, education, youth guidance and matters relating to health and welfare. At present, our budget limits our attention to Staten Island to one volunteer worker and one secretary. The cost of the two-year program we envisage would be $86,000.

I do hope it will be possible for you to meet with me. I am aware of the demands on your time and will keep our meeting brief.

Sincerely,

LETTER B

Dear Mr. ....:

Would you be kind enough to meet with me to discuss a special project which (Name of Agency) hopes to undertake, and in which

8

I think the ABC Foundation might be interested.

Briefly, it is a project which will enable this organization to provide local family casework service required as part of inter-country adoption procedure in the many American communities where it is now unavailable or inadequate, and where, as a result, local families cannot adopt children from abroad through any accredited agency. Its annual budget is $33,400.

I do hope you will wish to discuss this matter further with me and I look forward to hearing from you. For your information, I have enclosed a copy of our current Annual Report.

Sincerely,

The next two letters also request meetings to discuss special projects. Both come from organizations outside of New York City and both seek meetings with foundations in that city. Note, again, how specific the letters are. In the case of letter C, which was from a guidance agency in the mid-west, the project was already under way; thus, the letter contains a bit more detail. Note that the agency is willing to finance part of the cost of continuing the project from its own resources—frequently an important consideration with foundations.

LETTER C

Dear Mr. .... :

I am writing to request an appointment to discuss an important new project undertaken by (Name of Agency).

Briefly, it is an experimental Remedial Education Program—established as part of our total counseling process—for youngsters with severe cultural and educational handicaps. So that the Remedial Education Program could be more fully integrated into our counseling process, it is conducted directly on our premises. It is under the direction of a fulltime remedial specialist.

The Program was begun in March of this year. Even in so brief a period, it has resulted in dramatic improvements, not only in the reading, writing and arithmetic skills of many boys and girls, but also in the attitudes of these youngsters toward themselves and their society.

We do not have the required funds—$18,500—to continue the Program beyond this year. Were we compelled to abandon it at this time, it would be a deep loss to the youngsters whom we are helping—and those who will follow.

I plan to be in New York City during the period of October 8th through the 17th and would very much appreciate meeting with you at any point during that time. I shall look forward to hearing from you.

Sincerely,

LETTER D

Dear Mr. ....:

I am writing to ask whether you would be kind enough to meet with me briefly to discuss a project to provide casework counseling to American students in Paris, France. I will be in this country from May 1 through May 10 and would be available for such a meeting at any time during that period.

Counseling services to American students, for which there is an urgent and demonstrable need, would be made available through a central agency formed under the auspices of (Names of Agencies). The annual budget is $27,000. I believe the ABC Foundation may be keenly interested in this project, and I do hope it will be possible for you to meet with me.

Sincerely,

The next two letters were sent by a small denominational college, and a youth recreation agency. Both sought meetings to discuss what would, in effect, be a general purpose grant. But note how each letter, even in the brief space utilized, attempts to present a special circumstance justifying a grant. (This point is elaborated in the section on general purpose letters.) Note, also, the first paragraph of letter F, reflecting the fact that the writer has taken the trouble to ascertain that the foundation is particularly interested in his field.

10

Dear Mr. ....:

May I come to see you about some exciting developments that are taking place at XYZ College, where a committed faculty and an involved student body are working together to re-create an institution of learning that will be totally relevant to these changing times?

It is not often that a small private denominational college has the opportunity to demonstrate what can be done as a result of radical self-examination and a determination to depart from the past—however painful that may be—and move towards the future. We believe our experience can be helpful to other small colleges that must come to terms with today's educational realities.

Our school has been undergoing dramatic changes in every area of its operations. We have converted from a commuter college to one with resident students, have greatly strengthened our faculty and administration, and are in the process of completely revamping our curriculum.

Can a meeting be arranged within the next week or so to discuss the possibility of a grant in support of this program? My calendar can be readily arranged for a time suitable to you.

Sincerely yours,

LETTER F

Dear Mr. ....:

Knowing of the interest of the ABC Foundation in camping, I was wondering if I might call on you to discuss the work of (Name of Agency).

Specifically, I am hopeful that the Foundation might be willing to consider a grant to (Agency) to enable it to extend its unique camping program to an increased number of boys from New York City's ghettos during the summer of 19......

I shall not attempt to describe here the nature of (Agency)'s extensive camping program, except to indicate that it is considered one of the most distinguished in the country—particularly in its beneficial results with disadvantaged youth.

I do hope you will be willing to meet with me. I know how busy your schedule must be and I will keep our meeting brief.

I look forward to your reply.

Sincerely,

The next letter in this series is from an organization serving the mentally retarded. Note, particularly, the second paragraph. It indicates the overall amount required to purchase the new building, and, more significantly, shows that certain leading foundations have already given the building campaign their support.

Finally, it expresses the organization's confidence in its capacity to raise the full amount required provided matching support comes from the foundation area.

LETTER G

Dear Mr. ....:

May I meet with you to discuss the possibility of your Foundation granting funds to enable (Name of Agency) to purchase a building desperately needed to house and expand our programs for mentally retarded children?

We are seeking foundation support in matching funds in the amount of $500,000. At this point we have commitments of $100,000 from the ABC Foundation and $75,000 from XYZ Foundation. Once we achieve our goal from foundations, we have good reason to believe that we can raise the remaining funds within a six-month period.

I shall not attempt to detail here (Agency)'s varied and unique programs, except to note that this agency has in its brief fifteen years achieved a distinguished record in helping retarded children advance educationally and emotionally.

I do hope you will be kind enough to meet with me. I will keep our meeting brief.

I look forward to hearing from you.

Sincerely,

A fund-raising campaign if its going to last for any length of time should be considered a living, changing, dynamic entity, and the materials you use should change with it.

The next two examples—taken from a building campaign by an organization on the west coast—indicate how the nature and thrust of appointment letters can change to reflect the changed nature of the campaign.

Letter H shows the campaign very close to its beginnings. No more than 20% of the required funds have come in—and the important point is made that this represents board gifts. It is likely at this stage of the campaign that efforts are focused on securing grants very well into five figures and perhaps six.

Letter I shows the campaign in its closing stages. Ninety percent of the funds are now in—and now the effort is directed at getting that final, and sometimes, tough 10%. The point of this letter though is that success is in the air. Even a small foundation can see how significant its grant can be. The letter also offers a basis for going back to foundations which may have declined to make grants when the campaign was getting underway.

LETTER H

Dear Mr. .... :

May I meet with you to discuss the possibility of support from the ABC Foundation for a project that we at XYZ Agency consider to be of unusual importance?

Briefly, XYZ is planning to build in the heart of .... the nation's first arts workshop designed specifically for predominantly disadvantaged, multicultural population. Its objective is to offer, under one roof, a variety of arts programs of high quality that will have relevance to the diverse neighborhood groups: Chicano, black, white middle class, and Chinese.

XYZ Board members and their families have contributed, or pledged, $300,000 of the $1,500,000 needed to finance the workshop. This is about as far as we can go as a board. Now we must secure the help of public spirited foundations and friends in the community.

I would consider it a privilege if you would meet with me, and I will look forward to hearing from you.

Sincerely,

LETTER I

Dear Mr. .... :

After four years of planning—and 18 months of vigorous fund raising —XYZ Agency is on the verge of being able to construct the first arts workshop specifically designed for a predominantly disadvantaged, multicultural population.

We need just a little more help, and I am writing in the hope that you will meet with me to let me make our case for your support. Our goal is $1,500,000 for building and equipping the workshop. We have thus-far received in contributions and pledges $1,350,000. Our board gave $400,000 of the amount.

Our first concern is to raise the relatively small amount of money needed to go ahead with the building, and that is what I hope we will discuss. I would be most appreciative, if you would meet with me, and I shall look forward to hearing from you.

Sincerely,

The final example in this series differs from the others in that it is rather more detailed. On occasion you may feel for whatever reason that prospects for securing a meeting are very dim, or as in the case with the letter below, that the time span between when your letter will be received and when your project must begin may turn out to be too brief to allow for a meeting. It still pays to seek the meeting, but on the possibility that the foundation may be bound and deter- mined to make a decision, its a good idea to include a little extra information.

LETTER J

Dear Mr. .... :

Based on 15 years' experience, (name of agency) has planned a ven- turesome and, if we have the means to make it work, extremely worth- while project for this summer, and I hope that you and I can meet to discuss the possibility of assistance.

14

We intend to create (Agency) Clubs in two high schools—(names of schools)—where we have never before been able to gain entrance because of organized militant resistance and heavy acceptance by .... students of the mores of the drug culture. Each club will cost approximately $8,000 to establish and maintain for one year.

Our objectives are as follows:

- To counteract the negative self-evaluation and sense of personal frustration that causes more than 40% of .... high school students to drop out;

- To provide club members with self-motivation that can help them overcome disadvantages rising from a different language, an alien culture and a home oriented toward bare survival;

- To offer them the experience in self-government and the opportunity to achieve that has awakened in so many the realization that their own actions can alter the future.

Since 1956, (Agency) Clubs have had a profound impact on the youthful .... community. Then, approximately 120 .... entered college and most quickly dropped out. Last year, (Agency) clubs alone placed 835 in college with over $1,000,000 in student aid. We do offer a practical alternative to despair and violence—and now we feel ready to venture into areas of hardcore resistance.

Our community organizers must begin work within six weeks when school ends this year. With two months of summer work, a club can be functioning by September. We have the experience, we believe we know what to do and how to do it—now we must turn to agencies like the ABC Foundation for the seed-money to begin.

I look forward to hearing from you and greatly hope that you can fit a meeting into your busy schedule. With many thanks.

Sincerely,

Appeals For General Purpose Grants

There are, generally speaking, two kinds of grants secured from foundations; the first is for special projects, which we will talk about in the next section; the other is for general operating purposes.

Most agencies would rather have the second than the first. The reasons are obvious. A general operating grant may be used for any purpose designated by the agency. It enables the agency to take care of such unglamorous needs as paying its rent, its staff, the electric bill and keeping the place clean.

But, just as general purpose grants are more desired, so are they more difficult to come by, although not as difficult, incidentally, as some people think. Two recent surveys by Public Service Materials Center revealed that about half of the larger foundations (assets of over $500,000) do make general purpose grants. (Virtually all of the smaller foundations make general purpose grants.)

The point is that foundations, broadly speaking, do not make operating grants gladly or with enthusiasm. They do so usually when there are special circumstances justifying such a grant.

And those are the key words to remember when seeking such a grant—*special circumstances*: reasons above and beyond the values of your organization's ongoing program which merit a grant.

What are such reasons? Let's turn immediately to the first letter in this series. It was developed by a health agency in Staten Island, New York, and is, in the final analysis, no more than a request for general operating funds. Note, however, the many special circumstances that have been built into the letter.

The first paragraph immediately sets a tone of urgency, indicating that this is no ordinary appeal. This point is strongly established in the next two paragraphs, with some very graphic examples given to spell out the extent of the population increase that is taking place on Staten Island.

But a "population explosion," in itself, may not be entirely convincing insofar as its effect on the work of the agency is concerned. So the writer analyzes the nature of the anticipated population increase and is able to document that it will, indeed, very much affect the work of the agency.

What further special circumstances can this health organization offer about itself? 1) It is already running a deficit; 2) It possesses a quite small reserve; and 3) It will use the foundation's grant solely to meet operating deficits incurred in the expansion of service, and it will be a one-time grant.

Having made all these basic points, the letter is quickly concluded.

Dear Mr. .... :

I am writing to ask the ABC Foundation to help the XYZ Agency meet a crisis situation which may seriously impair our effectiveness in rendering full health and medical services in the coming years.

In brief, with the construction of the Verrazano Bridge, we are faced with a "population explosion" during this decade equal to the entire population increase that has taken place since we were established nearly forty years ago.

According to the U.S. Census Bureau projections, our population will leap from 222,000 to 350,000 within the next five years. (It is already increasing at the rate of more than 1,200 new people each month.) On this basis alone, our current annual rate of 30,000 visits will climb to over 45,000.

However, the problems we face in the years ahead are even more serious than indicated by the projected increase in case load. At present, forty per cent of our services are provided without charge. The nature of our new population indicates that the proportion of free services will almost surely rise—and, quite steeply.

For, according to Census projections, there will be a 300 per cent increase in our Negro population from 10,200 to 30,000 and a 600 per cent increase in Puerto Ricans from 2,500 to 20,000. Because such families and children have all too frequently not received proper health care, they are precisely the ones who will most need our health services. They will most likely also be the ones who will be most unable to pay even a minimal fee for such services.

We have enclosed our current Annual Report. As you will note, we ended the year with an operating deficit of $................... And this is *before* feeling the impact of the newly-arriving families. For this year, our expenses are budgeted at $.................... Without a proportionate increase in income, this means an operating deficit of over $................... for the current year.

It is my hope that the value and need for the health services of the XYZ Agency, in general, may already be known to you. (A brief description of the agency's various programs is given here.)

We recognize that we cannot hope to provide these services on their present level to the thousands of new families establishing residence on Staten Island. For this reason, we turn to you. Our Board of Directors has voted to establish a reserve fund with a goal of $................... to be used solely to meet operating deficits to be incurred in the expansion of services. Currently, we have less than $.................... Would the ABC Foundation consider making a *one-time* grant of $.................... to our reserve fund?

During the years ahead, the XYZ Agency faces the most difficult challenge it has ever been called upon to meet. It is a challenge that excites us, so great is the opportunity for increased services. And yet, it is also a challenge which we know we cannot meet alone.

Most earnestly, we appeal to the ABC Foundation for its favorable consideration of our request for support.

Sincerely,

The special circumstance in this letter—prepared by an organization working with crippled children — quite simply, is that a most useful program will die unless additional funds are forthcoming. Note, among other points:

- the reasonable explanation as to why funds are no longer available
- the assurance that the program can be made self-sustaining
- the use of third party endorsements
- and the invitation to observe the program at first hand.

Dear Mr. ....:

I am writing to ask the ABC Foundation to help us meet an urgent situation with regard to one of our most needed programs—our .... Program for children with multiple handicaps.

This program was undertaken four years ago through a bequest of $..................... Appropriations from this bequest will be exhausted by the end of the year.

We do not possess the funds to continue the program by ourselves and without the help of a substantial nature we shall be compelled to abandon it. The lives of the children already in the program—and those who will follow—have already been marked by deep tragedy. To these youngsters, this will be the final—the irrevocable—tragedy.

Because of the multiple nature of their handicaps, none of them are admissible into the public schools. Many of them are classified as uneducable, and, so, do not even receive homebound instruction. Virtually their only outlet to the world—the world of play, of companionship, of emotional growth, indeed, of even the most simple kind of happiness—is the .... Program.

Twice a week, for thirty weeks out of the year, we transport fifty-five such youngsters to and from .... Here they participate in a wide range of recreational and development activities. Because of the special nature of their handicaps, a one-to-one adult-child relationship is maintained. Sometimes the measure of a child's advance is the fact that he smiles and laughs for the first time in his life. Sometimes we have found that a judgment made with regard to a given child has been too harsh, that, given unlimited love, attention, understanding, and the required firmness, he can be reached, he can communicate, he can, in fact, take his first tentative steps to a richer, more varied life.

In a recent instance, a four-and-one-half year old boy, the child of blind parents, was admitted into the program. A cerebral palsied youngster, he had had virtually no social experience of any kind due to his family background. Before coming to the ...., he was classified as uneducable, with an IQ of below 50. We found, in fact, that he had a good basic intelligence, although the extremely limited nature of his social contacts had permitted no development of his mental capacities. He has now been admitted into our nursery-kindergarten for orthopedically handicapped children, who are otherwise normal. I do not think it would be an exaggeration to state that in this case the life of a small boy—if by life we mean something more than existence—was saved by the .... Program.

All this will be lost with the loss of the .... Program. For this reason, we most earnestly appeal to the ABC Foundation to provide the funds to enable us to continue this vitally needed service. As you will note on the enclosed budget, it costs in excess of $.................... to maintain the program annually.

The program has earned the high endorsements of leaders in the professional community as well as almost painfully embarrassing statements of appreciation from parents of the children. Samples of such endorsements are being sent under separate cover.

We ask that the ABC Foundation make a one-time grant to enable us to carry the program through the end of the year. We are developing plans for an expanded fund raising project of our own and are confident that we shall, thereafter, be in a position to conduct the .... Program on a self-sustaining basis.

We have attempted in the foregoing to communicate our urgent feeling with regard to the .... Program. We urge you, however, to visit our offices and see the program in operation for yourself. For we believe that no words—no matter how eloquent or deeply felt— can equal your own first hand observation in determining the value, the need and the hope that this program has for the children it serves.

Sincerely,

The next three examples were prepared respectively by an international child welfare organization; a youth guidance agency; and a neighborhood house.

They are quite different, yet they share one common bond. Each letter seeks to express special circumstances, reasons above and beyond the merits of the ongoing programs, as a means of justifying a grant.

In the letters that follow are such special circumstances as:

- expansion of services, with a still greater increase projected for the future
- operating deficit
- highest budget yet adopted
- the fact that a number of foundations have found the agency worthy of general support
- a significant anniversary date
- the experimental nature of organization
- a reason why foundation support in particular is sought.

Gentlemen:

I am writing to request a grant from the ABC Foundation in support of the work of XYZ Agency.

(Two paragraphs of background on XYZ Agency.)

It is significant that 19...... witnessed an increase in virtually every category of XYZ Agency services. Last year, XYZ Agency served over 7,500 cases involving some 32,000 people, an increase of 16% over the previous year. It is, I believe, of particular importance to note that 78% of this increased case load involved problems directly affecting the welfare of children.

Quite apart from the fact that we are hard-pressed to maintain services on an existing level, there is every indication that the demand for such services will be mounting even more steeply in the years to come, for indeed there has been occurring a very real "mobility explosion" of peoples throughout the world.

Last year, two million Americans resided or traveled abroad while, at the same time, one million foreign nationals came to the United States. As our world shrinks, XYZ Agency services, by definition, must expand. The very fact of the increasing mobility of people means an increasing need for intercountry case work. It means, in effect, an expanding need for the specialized skills of a professional agency deeply concerned for human beings in trouble, wherever they may be, with the understanding and the technical knowledge to bridge international barriers of differences in culture, as in language.

Within the framework of our limited resources, we are determined to meet that need. As one measure in doing so, our Board of Directors adopted for 19..... the highest operating budget in XYZ Agency history — $.............................. As an indication of what this means to us, our operating expenses for 19..... — just four years ago — were $........................

Many foundations have oriented themselves to supporting new projects. Others—and I most deeply hope the ABC Foundation is one— recognize also the need for supporting the maintenance and expansion of ongoing services that have already proved their usefulness. We take some pride in the fact that last year 57 foundations made grants totaling $.............................. to XYZ Agency for just this purpose.

Would it be possible for the ABC Foundation to make a grant of $.............................. to XYZ Agency for each of three years commencing with 19.....? We have begun an evaluation and strengthening of all aspects of our fund raising structure, and I am confident that we will not require your assistance beyond a three-year period.

Most deeply, I hope you will favorably consider this request. If you should require any additional information, I would be more than happy to furnish it.

Sincerely,

Gentlemen:

I am writing to request a grant from the ABC Foundation in support of XYZ Agency.

(Brief description of program)

As you can see, we are more than just a local counseling agency, important as that phase of our work is. Our pilot projects and special demonstrations have played, and continue to play, a leading role in advancing vocational guidance programs throughout the country.

I should like to add one more reason why I am particularly hopeful that you will favorably consider this request. Unlike many other charitable organizations, XYZ Agency does not possess a mass emotional appeal. This is true despite the fact that we are frequently involved in highly dramatic situations. There is, however, no easy slogan to express the difference between fulfillment in one's work and imprisonment in it—no simple photograph to show the crippling of the spirit by work without meaning, satisfaction or relationship to ability.

(Letter is concluded with a request for an annual grant for each of three years.)

Sincerely,

Gentlemen:

This is the 100th anniversary of XYZ Community Center, and we come to you in this landmark year, not to celebrate history, but to ask your support for important new programs that can, we hope, help to change the alarming trend toward destruction in our cities today.

The Center's traditional role has always been to bridge the gap between what is needed and what is provided, and now, as in the past, we have accepted our obligation to move boldly into areas of greatest stress. We have committed the technical resources and full facilities of the Center towards developing and testing new services that will serve a nation as well as a neighborhood.

We do this in the face of a projected deficit for 19...... of more than $............................ because we feel needs exist that cannot any longer be postponed. We hope the ABC Foundation will support this view with a grant towards the cost of our innovative programs to alleviate city ills.

The educationally disadvantaged, the unemployed and the unemployable, the second and third generation welfare family, the elderly poor

—these are the people who need us most, and I would like to tell you about some of the work we are now doing at XYZ Community Center to help them.

(A description of the programs of XYZ Community Center follows.)

But all of these things are being done at XYZ Community Center, not with the objective of affecting our neighborhood alone, but, also, with the goal of having an impact on New York's inner city and the inner cities of our nation. As you may know, throughout its 100-year history, XYZ Center has been regarded as a national laboratory, where services to meet human needs are tested, improved and passed along to others.

We turn now to the ABC Foundation at a time of crisis in our cities, but, also, at a time that XYZ Community Center, by way of its experience and commitment, is best able to play its role in helping to meet that crisis. Will the ABC Foundation help us? Would the Foundation consider making a grant of $.............................?

Our resources are now strained to the utmost, and such a grant would afford us an extra measure of stability in maintaining our programs while pioneering still new ones. Most earnestly, I hope you will favorably consider this appeal. Should you wish any further information, I would, of course, be delighted to furnish it. Or I and other officers of the Center would be glad to appear before your Board, if you should desire that.

Sincerely,

A request for a general purpose grant does not have to take the form of a letter. Your request can be made in normal presentation form, together with a covering note, as in the following example. Observe, here, the relative brevity of the request, and, also, that it involves basically the expansion of the existing program.

Dear Mr. .... :

On behalf of the Board of Governors of XYZ Agency, I am submitting herewith a request to the ABC Foundation for a grant of $9,500 to enable (Agency) to extend its unique camping facilities to 100 additional disadvantaged boys during the summer of 19......

We have made this request so soon after the close of the current season because we want to be certain, as we plan for next year, that no boy who turns to XYZ Agency will fail to find the help and guidance he requires.

Neeedless to say, if you wish any further information, I would be delighted to furnish it.

Sincerely,

This is a request to the ABC Foundation for a grant of $9,500 to enable XYZ Agency to extend its unique camping facilities to 100 additional boys from New York City's ghettos during the summer of 19......

The camping program of XYZ Agency serves over 3,500 boys each summer — more than any other single organization — and is regarded as one of the finest in the country. At our six modern resident camps, some of the city's neediest boys receive summer vacations that not only help build them physically, but also contribute to their moral and spiritual development.

The Problem: It costs XYZ Agency $95, not including capital expenditures, to provide two weeks of camping for one boy. Fees charged to our campers cover only a fraction of this cost — and most of their parents cannot afford to pay even these. The result is that our camps operate each year at a substantial deficit which we make up ourselves.

Thus, in seeking to increase the number of poverty level youngsters served by our camps, (Agency) must also seek new sources of income. It is in this connection that we have turned to the ABC Foundation, whose concern for the welfare of young people is too well known to require further citing here.

Facilities: Our camps are modern, well-appointed, and rank with the best in the country. This has been done advisedly. For the youngsters whom our camps serve have had too much previous experience in receiving leftovers; in having to make do with shoddy equipment, inadequate facilities and dilapidated accommodations. By giving them facilities that are the best that are available, we are able to provide a more complete camp experience and at the same time to heighten their sense of self worth.

The Camps' Programs: Our camps offer boys, 8 through 13 years of age, a two-week vacation during July and August. Most of these boys take part in our winter programs. Camping, therefore, becomes an extension of their city activities. For boys with special problems, this provides a continuity of individual help from a specially trained staff. At camp, boys enjoy a wide range of outdoor activities. These include: swimming, sailing, boating and other water sports, baseball, fencing, karate, music, art, acting, photography and campcrafts. Particularly valuable is the experience these young people get in group living, in learning to use the democratic process in planning activities, and the opportunity it offers them to develop leadership. Today, both the young campers and their parents are being involved in the planning of the camp program with the result that the activities have greater relevance to their lives.

An innovation at our camps in the 19..... season was a Leadership Development Program. Starting with a group of 45 boys who were beyond the camp age, XYZ Agency offered an apprenticeship in basic camp skills. These teenage neighborhood boys were able to earn while they learned how to be camp counselors and how to perform such camp skills as: food preparation, waterfront duties, serve as aides to program directors, help in purchasing, assist in the camp office, make simple repairs to camp buildings, and maintain the grounds.

Back in the city at the end of the camp season, all except two of the trainees continued their training at our community centers where they now serve as program aides. As a result of this opportunity, these boys — some of whom were school dropouts — are now back in school with a view to graduating, and several are even thinking about going to college.

Summary: We do not claim that there is anything dramatic or new about camping. But we do not know of a single other service to youth — new or old — that works as well. There is still no better antidote to the poisonous effects of poverty and neglect than taking children away from crowded slum neighborhoods and bringing them close to nature. By giving them a chance to experience outdoor living; by teaching them how to develop physical skills; and by helping them to know the satisfactions of teamwork and sportsmanship, we equip them to go back to their neighborhoods morally and spiritually stronger and better able to overcome the hazards of their environment.

For all of these reasons, we most earnestly hope that the ABC Foundation will find it possible to approve a grant of $9,500 to enable XYZ Agency to make its camping facilities available to 100 additional boys in the summer of 19......

The final general purpose appeal in this series illustrates still another special circumstance. A crest of publicity, not necessarily about the agency, but about the field of work in which it is involved can create events which warrant new or increased support from foundations. The alert agency takes advantages of such opportunities, as witness the following example.

25

This is a proposal to the ABC Foundation, requesting a grant of $6,000 to help XYZ Agency, a non-profit, non-sectarian agency, to meet the current crisis in home care for retarded children in the Chicago area. This grant would enable XYZ to employ an additional Home Aide for one year to provide on-the-spot assistance at home for six to eight families who have a retarded child and need help in coping with their family situation and in learning how they can help their retarded child develop his potential.

The Need for an Expanded Home Aide Program
Recent publicity about conditions suffered by retarded persons confined to the School has further increased the growing public and professional conviction that retarded children should be kept in a home setting wherever possible. Indeed, XYZ and other agencies agree that when children are given training and special assistance at home, especially during their early years, they are much better able to develop their potential and, in some cases, may approach normalcy.

This new emphasis on home care, plus the spreading word about the XYZ Home Aide program, has caused the agency to be so deluged with requests that, for the first time in its history, XYZ has been compelled to reluctantly set up a waiting list for service. But retarded children and their families cannot wait. The pressures of living with a retarded child, combined with other pressures of family life, can gravely disrupt a family which cannot get the help it needs. And every month that passes while a retarded child awaits special assistance lessens that child's chance to make headway.

Furthermore, XYZ cannot refer the families on its waiting list elsewhere for home aide assistance. Only a few agencies in Chicago offer any version of this service for retarded children, and only XYZ provides the service at cost that all families can afford; XYZ asks families to pay what they can afford on a sliding fee scale and charges nothing if they cannot afford to pay.

More About the XYZ Home Aides
Home Aides are English and Spanish-speaking women whom XYZ trains as paraprofessional staff workers to teach parent how to understand their retarded child's needs and to show them what they can do to fill these needs and stem their child's retardation. At the same time, the Home Aide helps families deal with day-to-day problems, whether or not they be directly caused by the presence of a retarded child in the home.

Home Aides are mature women with child care experience who are chosen for their patience, warmth, stability, understanding and tolerance of deviant behavior—qualities that are important in dealing with the parents as well as the retarded child. Because of her own background, the Home Aide is in a unique position to understand the family's lifestyle and interpret problems to the social worker. Thus the Home Aide also serves as a bridge between the parents and the social work staff which, in turn, provides professional counselling to preserve the family's emotional health.

A home aide generally works in the home of each of two families two or three days a week for three or four months. Thus, in one year, one home aide can serve six to eight families regularly, while providing emergency service to many additional families.

To Meet the Challenge
In its public education efforts, XYZ has done a great deal to dispel the image of the average retarded child as an unattractive, helpless "crib case" who must be shut away because nothing can be done to help him develop. On the contrary, XYZ has pointed out that 90% of children who are labeled "retarded" are only mildly retarded and can benefit enormously from home care.

Even if most of these children cannot become normal, home aide assistance can save them from institutionalization in later life, as well as in the early years; because of their development gains, many of these children will be able to find a place in the community, albeit perhaps a special and sheltered one, and thus will not have to be a burden to themselves, to their families or to the society which would otherwise have to finance their care in a public institution. (Today, a month's care in a public institution costs about $700.)

Furthermore, XYZ has found that even if a child eventually does need institutional care, he is much better off for his experience of family living and early home training. Indeed, a child can adjust more easily to, and profit more full from, institutional training if he has first received training at home.

Thus your grant of $6,000 would give a new lease on life to at least six to eight children in the coming year, and more in the years to come through the home aide position that you would help to create. Certainly, your generosity would make an invaluable contribution to urgently needed resources for the retarded at a time of unprecedented increase in the number of retarded children and their families needing and seeking the tremendous benefits of early home assistance.

27

Special Project Presentations

Rather than list a series of abstract rules for the writing of effective special project presentations, let's start this section by dealing directly with such a presentation.

The presentation that follows was prepared by a mid-western youth guidance agency. It deals with a project designed to render a particular service while — more importantly — developing new areas of knowledge.

The first item that meets the eye of the foundation official who will be reviewing the presentation is the covering note. It follows.

Dear .... :

On behalf of the Board of Trustees of (Name of Agency), I am enclosing herewith a presentation requesting a two-year grant from the (Name of Foundation) to finance a research project designed to determine whether concentrated counseling of "almost dropout" boys and girls can alter their decision to leave school.

The presentation speaks for itself. I would only add that this organization has high confidence not only in the direct benefits the project may provide to the youngsters who participate in it, but, also, in the national significance it may have.

Needless to say, we would be delighted to provide whatever additional information you might require. A copy of our current Annual Report is enclosed.

Sincerely,

Observe that the covering letter is rather brief, but that it manages to convey the essence of the project. Note, also, that although the tone is quite businesslike, the covering letter also communicates something of the excitement felt by the agency which hopes to undertake the project.

From this point, we move on to the presentation itself. The first page is the title page, and it is quite simple:

A Proposal To
(Name Of Foundation)
From
(Name Of Agency)

Now, for the presentation itself. It is quite important that the reader know as quickly as possible the essentials of your proposal. This is true for several reasons, not the least of which is that your presentation may be one of two or three dozen that arrived in the mail that morning.

Note the first two paragraphs:

This is a request to the (Name of Foundation) from (Name of Agency) for a two-year grant of $91,540 ($41,240 for the first year, $50,300 for the second), to finance a research project designed to determine whether concentrated counseling of "almost dropout" boys and girls in the critical months before they have dropped out can alter this course, together with improving their attitudes toward society in general and education in particular.

The project will be conducted in collaboration with three neighborhood high schools — (Names of Schools). It has the full approbation and enthusiastic support of the Board of Education, which has agreed to release the children from school to participate in the project for the period needed.

At this point, the presentation has communicated the purpose of the project, how much it will cost, how long it will last, and, in the second paragraph, a strong indication of its state of readiness.

Having presented this very broad picture, the writers are now prepared to introduce relevant detail, and this is done in the following section entitled

BACKGROUND

There already exists in this country a vast array of work orientation, training, educational and vocational counseling resources, both public and private, available to youths after they have dropped out of school. Useful as these services are, they represent, in a sense, locking the barn

29

after the horses have been stolen. As yet, no one has measured the effect that a full range of counseling services, such as those provided by our agency, may have in actually changing the decision to drop out of school.

The young people whom we propose to bring into our research project have been chosen for two reasons: First, because they are within a few months of being 16 years of age, the legal minimum at which they can drop out of school; and second, because, in the opinion of the school authorities, they are almost certain to make this choice. They have records of troublemaking, vandalism and truancy. They resent virtually all forms of authority, and they see schools and schooling, not as a gateway to economic advancement and independence, but as just another kind of authority.

Over a two-year period there will be four experimental groups each with 15 children, who will remain in the project for five months, with a new group then succeeding the former one. There will, at the same time, be an equal number of matching children in four control groups, each also succeeding the other. Throughout the five-month period, the youngsters in the experimental group will receive the concentrated and continuing force of counseling, both individual and group; work orientation in our Pre-Vocational Workshop; psychological testing; remedial education; and part-time job placement (where it is decided that this would be a helpful course for a particular boy or girl).

This will mean that the child who has felt that no one was interested or believed in him would have at least five persons exhibiting interest and faith in his ability to succeed.

What is learned in the course of this two-year experiment may be directly beneficial to the many thousands of potential dropouts in this country, and of value to the scores of public and private agencies concerned with the problems of this particular group.

Note how lean the writing is in the preceding section and how much information it has imparted. Within the space of about half a typewritten page, the writer has placed his project in perspective by indicating the overall framework in which it is being undertaken (first paragraph). He has introduced basic procedural steps, as well as the elements of the research design (second and third paragraphs), has presented a major justification for believing in the possibility of success for the project (fourth paragraph), and — very important — has spelled out the ultimate significance of the project (last paragraph).

At this point, most of the salient features of the project have been given or suggested and it is now time to go into its actual workings, and this appears, aptly enough, under the heading

HOW THE PROJECT WORKS

The boys and girls in the experimental groups will be referred to (Agency) by guidance counselors at each of the three schools. Briefly, these are the services which (Agency) will provide:

Individual and Group Counseling

The role of the counselor is to help his young clients make decisions which will be right and beneficial for themselves. He will meet with them individually at frequent sessions, striving, first of all, to win their trust and confidence. For only then can he move to the point of significantly altering their attitudes.

Counseling of the youngsters as a group will also be an integral part of the program. Here, peer-to-peer, with the (Agency) counselor as catalyst, the boys and girls will have an opportunity to explore their resentments against society and schooling. The atmosphere will be kept as permissive as possible, with no fear of retaliation from the authority figure — the counselor.

Psychological Testing

Psychological tests will be administered to the boys and girls in the project, as an aid to the counselor in understanding them more fully — particularly in regard to determining areas of strength, not of weakness.

Remedial Education

Youngsters who are weak in reading, writing or arithmetic will be encouraged to improve these skills under the instruction of a professional specialist in remedial education. Each child will receive individual instruction and each will work at his own speed. In addition to improving the academic capacities of such children, we have found that success in this regard will show a corresponding gain in their attitudes toward themselves and toward society. The Remedial Education Program is conducted directly on (Agency) premises, thus permitting us to observe continually the progress of each client, and to integrate our observations into the total counseling process.

Pre-Vocational Workshop

Also located on (Agency) premises is our Pre-Vocational Workshop. The Workshop is divided into separate work centers, equipped to reproduce the settings for which typical entry jobs are currently available.

One center, for example, is a "supermarket," with grocery-stocked

31

shelves and a cash register at a check-out counter. Another contains office equipment for white-collar jobs; typewriters, filing cabinets, addressograph, mimeograph, etc.

The Workshop, however, is not so much intended as a training center as it is a tool of the counseling process. As is true of remedial education, the boys and girls will proceed at their own pace while receiving constant help and encouragement from their instructor.

Thus, for these young people, easily frustrated and well experienced in disappointment, the gap between the undertaking of an assignment and its completion will be relatively brief. Success will come quickly, and with it — we anticipate — will come a willingness to tackle more difficult assignments, an increased readiness to accept the discipline of a learning situation, and — finally — a greater degree of confidence in themselves.

Job Development

When it appears useful, we will, with the assistance of a (Agency) Job Developer, place certain of the boys and girls in part-time employment. Insofar as is possible, these will be jobs which will represent a learning experience for the youngsters and, in addition, give them a sense of self-esteem that goes with having earned their own money. Also, their experiences at work — positive or negative — will be useful subject matter for individual or group counseling sessions.

If all the details of the operation of the project had been included in the previous section, it would have slowed the narrative flow. Hence, another section follows, headed, simply,

OTHER DETAILS

It should be stressed that the keynote of the project will be its informality and flexibility, with each activity aimed at meeting the particular needs of each child. We are quite certain that if we are to involve these boys and girls in the total counseling process, they must first be involved on their own terms. Thus, these youngsters, in coming to (Agency), will bypass the usual intake procedure and meet their counselor directly. Even here, actual interviewing may not take place at the onset. Rather, if the counselor thinks it desirable, he may immediately introduce his client to the Pre-Vocational Workshop. If the client wishes to spend his first day in the Workshop, this is what he will do.

Psychological testing will be presented to the child as a means of *his* learning more about himself. And within a given range of tests, the client will be permitted to choose those he wishes to take.

It is both our goal and expectation that the child will spend three to four hours per day in the counseling process. However, we conceive this as an average, and will not insist on a prescribed number of hours for each day. Awakening a child's enthusiasm successfully can lead him to putting a long day of intensive effort which cancels out a day or two of non-attendance.

It will be noted, incidentally, that we have included in the budget provision for funds to buy lunches for the youngsters, since the time they spend at (Agency) usually will bridge the lunch hour. Also, the budget covers bus fares to and from (Agency).

We believe that the process described above — flexible, adapted to the needs of each youngster, and offered to him in terms that he can understand and accept — can indeed change attitudes, can replace alienation from society with a desire to be a part of it.

Note that the thrust of this section, as was true of the previous one, is designed both to provide relevant information and also to communicate that the originators of the project have full control of the elements involved. Thus, the sense of the feasibility of the project is heightened.

Now, because this is a research project, the elements involved in the research design and the means by which the project will be evaluated must be described. This is done in the following section, entitled

RESEARCH AND EVALUATION

The tools for evaluating the effectiveness of the project are self-evident. As we indicated, there will, over a two-year period, be four experimental and four control groups, each composed of 15 boys and girls, all a few months short of them 16th birthday.

By comparing each of the experimental and control groups we can then answer such basic questions as:

- How many within each group elected to stay in school when they reached the age of 16?
- Of those who stayed in school, was there any significant variation in their school records by way of both grades and behavior?
- Of those who dropped out of school, to what extent did they seek to improve their vocational readiness by enrolling in special governmental or private training programs?

Since this is a research project — and we ourselves shall learn from it — we shall also be concerned with putting the knowledge gained with each experimental group into effect with the one that succeeds it. Thus, within the four experimental groups, we shall make comparisons — as indicated above — to ascertain whether any new elements we may have added are significant in improving the overall results.

At the end of the two-year experimental period we shall publish a report covering the record of the project, together with our findings and conclusions. The report will be disseminated widely to professionals, to schools, and to agencies, both public and private, concerned with the dropout problem.

The last paragraph of this section is important in that it indicates that the organization undertaking this project does have a plan for disseminating the information it has gathered. It is unnecessary at this time to be more specific. One might mention, incidentally, that if this were a presentation which sought governmental funding, there would then be a need for greater detail. Foundations, however, do not require a similar range of particulars.

All that remains by way of narration, at this point, is a summary. The purpose of the summary is to communicate the essentials of the project in the most positive manner possible. In essence, it is the final opportunity to "sell" the project.

SUMMARY

The 60 boys and girls who will participate in this experiment are a microcosm. Nationally, their numbers can be multiplied many thousands of times over. In terms of the country's birth rate, this estranged element of society represents a booming area of population growth. Once they drop out of school, they are — from all statistics — well on their way to becoming a burden to themselves and to the country, idle and frustrated, with a high potential for crime and violence.

By concentrating on the narrow period of decision before these teenagers drop out, we believe the process may yet be reversed. We believe that the vigor and energy so characteristic of the youngsters may ultimately be directed into useful, productive channels — for the good of these boys and girls — for the good of the country.

To these ends we respectfully request the support of the (Name of Foundation).

The next item, of course, is the budget. It should appear on a separate page. For some reason, many grant seekers run afoul on the budget page.

Here is a basic rule of thumb you should remember in preparing your budget. The budget is a picture — in dollars and cents — of the total project. If your budget contains expenses of substance for items that are not covered in your written presentation — something is wrong with the picture. Conversely, if you have indicated in the written presentation anything that will cost money — services, facilities, travel, etc. — and have not presented these expenses, reasonably itemized in the budget — the picture is equally wrong.

Since this is a two-year project, note, also, that the budget allows for normal salary increments during the second year — a point sometimes overlooked by grant seekers in preparing their budgets.

PROJECT TO PROVIDE COUNSELING TO "ALMOST DROPOUT" STUDENTS

TWO-YEAR BUDGET

	First Year	Second Year
Counselor, full-time	$10,400	$11,000
Remedial Instructor, half-time	4,500	4,800
Job Developer, one day per week	1,800	1,900
Workshop Assistant, half-time	3,800	4,000
Secretary, full-time	6,000	6,500
Social Security Taxes	1,040	1,100
Research and Evaluation	3,000	3,000
Transportation and Lunches for Clients	3,500	3,500
Consumable workshop, testing and remediation materials	2,000	2,000
Writing, Printing and Distribution of two-year report	—	7,000
Administrative Overhead, including rent, supplies, telephone utilities, postage, etc.	5,200	5,500
Total	$41,240	$50,300

Total for two years: $91,540

35

Having reviewed one sample presentation, certain elements in the effective writing of such presentations should be apparent. Obviously, any sound presentation will include such basic points as the length of the project, its objectives, how it will operate, why it is needed and how much it will cost. The language describing these points should be as clear and simple as possible. By way of structure, the more important — or basic — information is given at the beginning of the presentation; the supporting details follow. Finally, the presentation should be kept brief — usually no more than five single-spaced typewritten pages, including neither the title page nor the budget page.

Obviously, the need for being brief can be overdone. Some things simply cannot be stated adequately within a limited amount of space (although it's a good idea, in these cases, to investigate whether a considerable body of the material cannot be presented in appendices); nor is being brief the same as being good. It is just as possible to be verbose, dull or illogical in a few pages as it is in many. Notwithstanding these strictures, the following is an example of a good, brief presentation prepared by an international child service agency.

Note how much information is communicated about the project in the opening paragraph, how only the relevant details are included. The presentation clearly establishes the need for the project, and, equally clearly, how the project would meet the need. Actually, in manuscript, the narrative portion of the presentation covered less than two typewritten pages.

This is a request from (Name of Agency) to (Name of Foundation) for a grant of $33,800 to launch the first year's operation of a new and unprecedented field service unit under our agency's direct auspices. Such a unit will make possible, for the first time, provision of local family casework service, required as part of inter-country adoption procedure in the many American communities where it is now unavailable or inadequate and where, as a result, local families are unable to adopt children from abroad through any accredited agency. Filling this service gap will enable many more American families who keenly wish to take foreign children into their homes to do so, and will open new opportunities for foreign children to find adoptive homes in the United States. At the same time, it will significantly help to foster greater awareness and understanding among community agencies in many parts of this country about the growing need for international cooperation and service in the field of family and child welfare.

THE NEED

(A one-paragraph description of the agency appears here.)

A particularly crucial area of service is that of inter-country adoption. Since 19....., (Agency) has made it possible for 24,000 foreign children, orphaned by war or personal family tragedy, to find stable, loving homes in the United States; and enabled a like number of childless American families to know the fulfillment of parenthood.

At this very moment, many hundreds of additional families are equally eager to open their homes and hearts to children from abroad — equally able to provide the kind of homes these children desperately need. Yet the channels of inter-country adoption are closed to these families — closed for the simple but tragic reason that in their home communities, there are no local agencies able to cooperate with us to arrange professionally safeguarded child placements.

Some of these areas comprise a single city — as, for example, Cleveland, Ohio. Some are county-wide — as, for example, Suffolk County, New York. Some cover portions of an entire state, as in Massachusetts; or even the state itself, as in Florida. All are highly populated areas, from which each year many families write us, seeking to adopt foreign childen; but without the cooperation of a local agency able to undertake the necessary on-the-spot investigations and provide direct casework service to the family, we are unable to help.

THE PLAN

In order to meet these families' needs, and to serve a still larger number of the homeless children abroad who depend on us for help, we propose to establish a field service unit. This unit would consist of two professionally trained and experienced caseworkers, whose headquarters would be our national offices in New York City, but who could be dispatched wherever and whenever needed to work on the local level with prospective adoptive parents. The field caseworkers would handle all investigative studies and casework for families in communities which are currently pockets of non-service. They would also work with and supplement the resources of local agencies in other communities where, despite the agencies' willingness to cooperate, their present heavy caseloads necessitate waiting periods of up to a year before families seeking inter-country adoptions can be served.

The executive staff of (Agency) in New York will direct all activity of the field unit; and will make use of its relationships with executives of local social service agencies in all communities to which field caseworkers may be sent, in order to explain their function, and lay the groundwork for the fullest possible cooperation.

In this way, not only can immediate and urgent service needs be met; but, in addition, agencies in what are now, from our standpoint, non-service or minimum-service communities, can become better informed about inter-country social work problems and procedures, and the great and growing need for their help in this area.

We believe this project can be of the utmost significance to prospective adoptive parents and to the children overseas whom they seek to adopt. We earnestly request your support.

(Followed by budget page)

The two preceding presentations dealt with projects that were wholly new to the agencies concerned. In effect, they were additions to the normal operations of each of the agencies.

Projects like these, even when financed by outside sources, can sometimes cause problems. They do little, if anything, to pay for on-going expenses, and, when completed, they may have proved so beneficial that the agency concerned is loath to give them up — except that it no longer has the financing to continue them.

Sometimes, an alert agency will examine its *existing* program to determine to what extent it may be possible to "project-ize" it, or, in the words of the following presentation, make it "larger than itself."

Obviously, this means adding a research component; it means seeking new knowledge; it means, in the final analysis, securing a good result which can be multiplied many times over.

Observe how all of these elements were integrated in this special project presentation from a social service agency located in a depressed section of a large urban center.

This is a request from the XYZ Association for a grant of $................................
to finance a comprehensive program of summer activities for 300 Harbury children and to make possible a study of the Summer Activity Program which may eventually benefit thousands of other Harbury children.

The 300 Children

The 300 children who are to be included in our proposed program of summer activities typify, in miniature, the total picture of children in

Harbury. Many come from broken homes. They have known neglect, racial intolerance, and the grinding pressures of bitter poverty. Some have already been in trouble with the law — on occasion, quite serious trouble. Others, somehow, have emerged relatively untouched by the corroding influences which permeate their daily lives and give promise of developing into mature, productive adults.

The 300 children are Negro, Puerto Rican and Italian, representing the three dominant groups in Harbury. Some come from poor families who live in clean, low-cost public housing. Others, equally poor, are jammed into unspeakably vile, deteriorating private tenements.

Schools in Harbury are far too crowded for the children to receive any kind of individual attention. Recreational facilities are virtually nil. Life is difficult for these children all year round. It is almost intolerable in the summer. For this is the time of boredom, of restless energies, of no place to go and no money to spend. It is a time when, almost against his will, a child may easily drift into trouble. Normally, only about 5 per cent of Harbury's 30,000 school age children get out of the hot city during the summer. The percentage will be even smaller this year. One of our leading agencies is in the process of reorganization and has closed down its summer camp.

Thus, at a time when these youngsters most need help, they are least likely to receive it.

We believe that our Summer Activity Program will do much to ease the problems faced by at least 300 Harbury children. We believe, further, that the program may prove larger than itself in reversing the tide of apathy and neglect running against thousands of other children in Harbury.

SUMMER ACTIVITY PROGRAM
Three Special Projects

We propose to undertake the following three special projects for 300 Harbury children. Budgets for each project are indicated on the final page.

Project One — Combined day camp and group work program for 240 pre-teen and teenage children.

Many Harbury children have never crossed the boundaries that divide the community. Few, if any, have ever been outside the city limits. To these youngsters the world is a place of stone and asphalt, of crowded streets pulsating with traffic, of ugly concrete and steel structures. In this close, confined world, children, even early in life, acquire values as hard as the world in which they live.

Through our combined day camp and group work program, we hope to introduce these children to a more gentle, spacious world — the world of the outdoors. We believe that days spent under the wide sky, among trees, and in grassy fields, must exert a profound influence both in body and soul. Divided into groups of 60, each child will spend two weeks at our day camp for which the Department of Parks has already agreed to allocate an out-of-the-city site. We will attempt to bring to our day camp many of the values found in residence camps. It will be conducted from Monday to Friday from 9:00 A.M. to 5:00 P.M. The children — Italian, Negro and Puerto Rican — will share in the whole gamut of exciting new experiences offered by the outdoors, from learning to swim to exploring nature, from gardening to picnicking to just lying in the sun. Together with this, there will be special trips to new places. A nominal fee of $5.00 per week will be charged the families of children attending the day camp. For those families who cannot afford even this token charge, the cost will be borne through our Scholarship Fund. The Association will furnish free milk to the children.

Two weeks out of the summer is not a very long time. Therefore, we propose to take care of the children during the remaining summer weeks through our group work program. Some of the activities of the group work program will take place within the Association itself. Here, the children will engage in a variety of games and creative pursuits including:

- Producing and acting in dramatic skits
- Group singing
- Woodworking
- Painting
- Planning for special events
- Story hours

A majority of activities of the group work program, however, will be conducted out-of-doors. Special trips will be made to interesting and colorful points in our city. In addition, visits will be made to city pools and to places where the children can fish and climb trees. Other trips will be arranged so that they can be undertaken jointly by parents and children, thus bringing the family unit a little bit closer.

As will be the case with all the projects, there will be a thorough check of the immediate effect and of any carry-over effect of this program upon the children.

Project Two — Evening recreational program and trips for 50 teenagers.

This program has a dual purpose. It will make the XYZ Association available to teenagers several evenings a week for social functions, athletics, arts and crafts, group singing, etc. We believe that, by filling boredom laden hours with healthy, wholesome activities, this element alone would justify support of the program.

Much more important, however, is the fact that the program will serve as a springboard for the planning and undertaking of weekend trips far out of the city — to Canada, through New England and to Washington, D.C.

One gains a frightening insight into the minds of Harbury teenagers in getting their impressions of travel outside of the city. Some actually fear that it would be a highly dangerous undertaking, that they risk being attacked by gangs, if not by the police themselves. Others are convinced that no hotel would open its doors to them and, if one did, only the most barren, depressing accommodations would be available. Certainly they would not be welcome.

In part, this tragic self image is due to the environment in which they live. Police brutality and gang warfare are anything but unknown in Harbury.Why should things be different elsewhere? In part, it is due also to the fact that children in our community do not have available to them the cultural experiences that are taken for granted by more well-to-do families. Harbury children rarely go on trips. Their jungle has at least the advantage of being theirs. They have little reason to think they are not surrounded by denser, more hostile jungles.

We believe that the opportunity of undertaking long trips — of living new experiences and of broadening their scopes both of people and places — must do much to help these children change their image and evaluation of themselves. In addition, their own conception of their own value increases almost unconsciously as they learn to plan and spend their own money on a variety of activities beyond the purchase of sweaters and jackets which is a typical teenage fund raising goal.

Project Three — Summer work program for 10 teenage boys.

The word, "job", has many meanings to Harbury teenagers. On the one hand, it means being able to acquire things of one's own. In a materialistic society, the children feel doubly a lack of material things. It has a deeper significance, too, sometimes unconsciously expressed by the children. Having a job means having a place — an identity — in the world. It means becoming an active, respected member of society, able to fill one's needs while serving a useful purpose. It would be difficult to express how profoundly our teenagers yearn to achieve this goal.

A job, however, also has negative connotations. For one thing, many teenagers associate work with the dull, unsatisfying drudgery that is frequently the lot of their parents. The idea that the fruits of one's work can be a source of pride is not easily accomplished.

Moreover, while teenagers yearn to become a part of society — and express this need through a desire to work — they also have an abiding dislike of society. Possibly this distrust begins with just living in Harbury where nothing comes easily and one has to fight hard to retain what one has. It continues in overcrowded schools that fail to satisfy an individual's interest and ability. Its culmination is in a deepseated insecurity. An obvious manifestation is a feeling of some teenagers that, when payday comes, they will somehow be shortchanged. In their minds, society has cast them in the role of victims. They are both fearful and resentful. Accordingly, we, at XYZ Association, felt it to be one of our major tasks to devise an occupational program in keeping with our teenagers' physical and intellectual abilities. Such a program would simultaneously offer personal guidance and occupational experience, service to the community, and an income commensurate with actual work performance and a young person's needs.

We believe that we have fulfilled all these requirements in our special work program for teenage boys.

In no sense will this be made "work". On the contrary, it will be quite important and necessary. We are converting several rooms within our building into a Theater Arts Center to be used for cultural activities and entertainments for children and adults throughout the Harbury community. Under the direction of qualified personnel trained in both vocational skills and group work, our teenagers will be responsible for building our theater. The work of the youngsters will range from constructing the stage to repainting chairs and tables. A storage room will be put into order. Easels, shelves and closets will be built, scraped, painted and polished. The boys will work six hours per day, five days per week and will be paid $2.50 per hour.

In the process of completing the job, the teenagers will learn work skills that will stand them in good stead throughout their lives. Add to this that they will have created a better XYZ Association for themselves and their friends. Add to this, also, that the product of their handiwork will constantly be there for them to see and take pride in. And, finally, add to all this that they will have been *paid* for their work.

We feel that there must be a significant gain in self-confidence and in self-respect for each of the teenagers. We feel, also, that they will be better equipped to cope with the problems which they and their community must still face.

The Study

As was noted, the 300 children who will participate in our proposed Summer Activity Program are more or less typical of most of the children living in Harbury. Consequently, it is reasonable to expect that the effect the Summer Activity Program has on these youngsters would be similar to the effect it would have on the great mass of Harbury boys and girls were they given the opportunity to take part in a like program. It is also reasonable to suppose that changes in the previously established patterns of behavior and attitudes of the 300 children, of which we have full knowledge, will be due to the impact of the Summer Activity Program.

We propose, therefore, to make an intensive study of the effect of the program upon the children. Specifically, the study will concern itself with these major areas:

- How does the rate of delinquency during the summer months of children who take part in the project compare with the rate of delinquency in Harbury as a whole?
- Will there be any effect on the rate of delinquency on children in the summer Activity Program as compared to their previous records?
- Will the children in the program show more positive attitudes toward themselves and their community as evidenced through direct, constructive actions?
- Will there be an improvement in racial attitudes of children in the program?
- Does participation in the project have a long-term effect? Six months after the program is completed, will the rate of delinquency of children who participated be less than the overall rate in Harbury? Will the records of the children themselves at the end of 19...... be better than they were at the end of 19......?

The study will be under the supervision of a trained research coordinator. He will be responsible for devising questionnaires when needed, for directing and coordinating interviews, for presenting the observations of group leaders, and for conducting follow-up studies. His reports will be transmitted to the ABC Foundation.

It may be that the results of our study will be negative, that there will be no appreciable difference among our 300 children in any of the

43

areas previously cited. In this case, we will have tried an experiment that failed. It will then be our task to re-evaluate our programs and to devise other programs that will be truly productive. Thus, even in failure certain values will emerge.

If, on the other hand, the study of our Summer Activity Program should reveal that the program has been a substantial success, we will probably be able to answer such questions as:

• What would our community have saved in dollars and cents alone if the Summer Activity Program had taken in, not 300 Harbury children, but 3,000? Or 10,000?
• How many serious crimes could have been prevented?
• To what extent could flare-ups due to racial antagonism have been forestalled?
• How many children might have contributed to the betterment of our community rather than toward its decline?

With this information in hand, we are confident that we can secure greatly increased support from community leaders for expanded Summer Activity Programs as will be the case with other agencies similar to ours. We are confident, also, that the mass communications media will cooperate fully in disseminating our study thus substantially increasing public understanding and support.

In the final analysis, we think that the Summer Activity Program — and the study thereof — may hold the seeds from which a sick, troubled Harbury can begin its growth into a more healthy, wholesome community.

To this end we appeal for your support.

The best time to seek foundation funds for a special project is *before* you undertake the project. This is true for a number of reasons. Foundations, as a group, prefer to support that which is new. Obviously, a project, once begun, has lost some of its claim to newness and, therefore, a certain amount of favor in the eyes of foundation decision makers. More basically, however, a project that has already established its usefulness, or proved its experimental point, is, as far as many foundations are concerned, no longer a special project, but rather just another facet of an organization's ongoing program.

Sometimes, however, a project does indeed get under way, proves its usefulness, and then runs out of financing before it reaches its final objectives. If the decision is made to look for foundation support, the best way to do so in a presentation is to give a frank accounting of

44

how the initial funds were secured and how they were spent, together with an explanation as to why the still required funds cannot be obtained from the original sources. Also, the consequences of not being able to complete the project should be indicated.

A religious school for the deaf was faced with this problem. Following is the successful presentation prepared by the school.

This is a request from XYZ School to the ABC Foundation for a grant of $15,000 for each of three years. The purpose of the grant is to finance the preparation, publication and distribution of three special teaching workbooks required to complete a unique and urgently needed set of religious educational materials: materials designed to make available to critically hearing-handicapped children — for the first time — a comprehensive inter-denominational course of instruction in the primary elements of Christian belief, presented in the simple words and slow step-by-step ways which alone can break through these children's difficult learning barrier.

No such set of materials, developed under Protestant auspices, now exists.

The Need The total development — mental, physical and spiritual — of the total child: this is a goal to which our society long ago concluded, any valid educational program must be committed. It is a goal to which our society is dedicated, not just for some of its children, but for all. But it is also a goal whose realization has presented unusual and almost insuperable difficulties for the parents and teachers of one tragically special group of children in our country — the deaf.

There are approximately three million children in the United States today whose hearing is seriously impaired. Many have been born deaf; others have become deaf in the first years of childhood — the crucial years when the language foundations are normally laid for a lifetime of acquiring knowledge through words. For these children, the result is a double — a learning, as well as hearing — handicap. A partial measure of the gap this handicap sets between a hearing and a non-hearing child may be seen in one simple statement: the average hearing child who enters first grade can understand and use (though not yet read) from 4,000 to 6,000 words — while the vocabulary of a deaf child entering school is literally non-existent.

This gap can be closed. But to do so requires time, patience, and highly skilled and sensitive teaching techniques evolved over many years of dedicated experimentation. It also requires educational materials specifically adapted to these teaching techniques. Thanks to the cumulative efforts of hundreds of specialists in the field of education for the deaf, such materials have been developed in most basic areas of the primary school curriculum; and accordingly, parents and teachers working to make possible a deaf child's normal mental and physical development no longer lack for help.

But if they are equally concerned for the child's spiritual development — if they want for him the same knowledge, understanding and joyful awareness of God in his life which a normal child absorbs effortlessly from home and church — then, suddenly, they are on their own. Help has been unavailable — because until less than a decade ago, not even an attempt had been made to develop religious educational materials for deaf children comparable to those in other subject-matter areas.

For families to whom the presence of God is immediate and daily sustenance, and for whom the knowledge of God informs all other knowledge, the helplessness they feel in trying to communicate their religious heritage is one of the sharpest they know. For their children, deprivation of the heritage means still another barrier between them and the world other children know — one more impediment, and not the least crucial one, to growth into whole and fulfilled adulthood.

The need for special means to ensure deaf children's development spiritually, as well as mentally and physically, is real. It has been too long unmet. A pioneering step directed at meeting it, at last, was taken in 19..... by XYZ School.

Our Answer Early in 19....., the School began development of a six-volume set of workbooks in the elements of the Christian faith, planned for the specific use of parents and teachers of deaf children, and scientifically scaled to these children's learning limitations.

The format of the series uses bright, appealing illustrations to clarify a carefully chosen vocabulary of simple words. They advance in maturity from book to book, with each volume supplying the foundation for approximately one year's instruction. The content of the complete series will progress from the presentation of basic religious concepts in the early volumes to, in the later ones, the explanation of essential points of doctrine shared by and expressed in the great Christian creeds.

(Title of workbooks as well as statement that they are first of their kind appears here.)

Of the six volumes, which have been developed as a unit though usable separately, three — Books I, II and IV — have been published.

The response to their appearance has been dramatic. Already 9,000 copies of the three books in print have been requested by organizations and schools for the deaf (both private and state-supported) in 43 states and nine foreign countries; while letters from parents and educators alike have flooded our office to convey their writers' approval, their gratitude, and their urgent requests for additional material. Letter after letter has said, like this one:

"Thank you for making workbooks in Christian religion available for deaf children, and we anticipate other workbooks for the older children."

Or like this one:

"Such an attractive and well planned workbook. I have shown the book to a number of teachers since I received it . . . All were highly impressed and hoped you would keep up the good work."

Or like these:

"The Staff has been most pleased with this material, and it is being used extensively . . ."

"An excellent workbook . . ."

"An asset . . ."

"Most helpful . . ."

And professional journals in the field of deaf education have noted these first volumes' availability with equal enthusiasm. Here are comments appearing in two leading publications:

(Quoted comments appear here.)

All three of the published volumes are being sent to you under separate cover.

The Problem In view of the demonstrated need for these materials, the insight and skill that have already gone into the planning of the full six-volume course, and the eager, inundating response that has marked the publication of the first books, it would be tragic, indeed, if this unprecedented educational project were to be broken off for lack of funds to continue it — yet this is the immediate prospect we face.

Volume I of the workbook series was underwritten through a special gift of the Trustees of the XYZ School; Volume II, as a project of the (name of religious women's organization); Volume IV, by an urgent one-time appeal to friends whose generous support also makes possible the existence of the School itself. Obviously, we cannot endanger the financial base on which our primary program, the School, depends by calling on these private sources of income for still more help.

47

Nor can we realize any revenue from sales of the three books already published. Approximately 70% of deaf children are taught in tax-supported state schools, which are prohibited by law from using public funds to buy religious educational materials — even though religious education may be provided in such schools on an equal-time or other basis. These legal restrictions mean that if any charge were made for the workbooks, it would no longer be possible for them to reach this group — the largest number of the deaf children who need them. Accordingly, we have no choice but to continue supplying the books free of charge, with the ironic result that as the demand for the books increases, so do our costs.

With these sources of support removed, all that we *can* do — and what we must do — is to seek new friends among foundations informed and concerned in the field of religious education, who will understand the importance of the work we have begun. For this reason, we have turned to the ABC Foundation hoping that because you understand our work, you will also want to help assure its completion.

Our Background   (Several paragraphs give background of school.)

Into the creation of this project has gone from 12 to 18 months of intensive work by the editorial committee on each completed volume so far, the accumulated experience of many professional lifetimes, and a commitment to God and to His children which, we deeply feel, must not be relinquished. The work so demonstrably well begun — so demonstrably and acutely needed — must not be left unfinished.

Its completion, and the spiritual foundations of many thousands of children's future lives, depend upon your help.

We shall hope and pray for your sympathetic and favorable consideration of our request.

Among the contributors to the aforementioned religious school for the deaf were several large foundations who — as it happened — gave relatively small amounts. It was decided to approach these foundations for support of the workbook project.

Obviously, the approach to a contributing foundation should not be the same as that to a foundation which is wholly new to your organization. Note, then, the differences in the two approaches by this school. The appeal to contributing foundations is much briefer; it takes the form of a letter; and the tone is considerably warmer. Also, a new element appears in the letter; an offer to honor or memorialize the gift. At the same time, however, the letter leaves the foundation ample opportunity to decline this public expression of appreciation.

Dear ....:

The ABC Foundation has been a warm and generous friend to XYZ School for several years and I write, now, to ask for your support in meeting an urgently important need.

The need is for help in financing the preparation, publication and distribution of three special workbooks required to complete a unique and indispensable set of religious educational materials: materials designed to make available to critically hearing-handicapped children — for the first time — a comprehensive inter-denominational course of instruction in the primary elements of Christian belief, presented in the simple words and slow step-by-step ways which alone can break through these children's difficult learning barrier. No such set of materials, developed under Protestant auspices, now exists.

In the absence of religious educational materials comparable to those in other subject-matter areas, parents have found themselves helpless to share their religious heritage with their hearing-handicapped children. For many families, this helplessness is one of the sharpest they know. For their children, deprivation of the heritage means still another barrier between them and the world of other children — one more impediment, and not the least crucial, to growth into whole and fulfilled adulthood.

A pioneering step to answer this need was taken by XYZ School in 19...... Early that year, the School began development of a six-volume set of workbooks in the elements of the Christian faith, scientifically planned for the specific use of parents and teachers of deaf children. Using bright, appealing illustrations to clarify a carefully chosen vocabulary of simple words, the lessons advance in maturity from book to book — progressing from the presentation of basic religious concepts in the early volumes to, in the later ones, the explanation of essential points of doctrine shared by and expressed in the great Christian creeds.

Of the six volumes, designed as a unit though usable separately, three — Books I, II and IV — have been published. The response to their appearance has been dramatic. Already 9,000 copies of the three books in print have been requested by organizations and schools for the deaf (both private and state-supported) in 43 states and nine foreign countries; while letters from parents and educators alike have flooded our office to convey their writers' approval, their gratitude, and their urgent requests for additional material. Professional journals in the field of deaf education have noted the first volumes' availability with equal enthusiasm.

Obviously, it would be regrettable indeed if this unprecedented project were to be broken off for lack of funds to continue it — yet this is the prospect we face. We exhausted our regular sources of support in financing publication of the first three volumes. Nor can we realize any revenue from sales of the books already published — were a charge to be made, the workbooks could no longer legally be used in the religious instruction programs of tax-supported state schools for the deaf, and thus could not reach 70% of the deaf children in this country who need them. Our only recourse is to turn for support to foundations such as yours.

As a matter of policy, our Board has decided to present publicly to the individual or foundation who most substantially aids in bringing the workbook project to completion our Humanitarian Service Award — established to honor men and women who most notably advance work in behalf of the hearing-handicapped. However, please let me add that should you not wish us to express our thanks to you in this way, we will, of course, entirely respect your feelings.

We shall hope and pray for your sympathetic and favorable consideration of our request.

Sincerely,

P. S. I have attached our budget for completion of the religious workbook series. I am sending you, under separate cover, copies of three completed volumes.

Many projects — perhaps most — are intended to last for more than one year. Few foundations, however, will commit themselves for more than one year. This is not to say that they will not fund the same project beyond that period. Usually, they will. But they will require a report on the first year's operation before proceeding to the second, and on the second year before going to the third.

Here is an example of such a report, prepared by a guidance agency as its project completed its second year.

Observe that the tone is objective, although there is no hesitancy in noting and expanding upon positive results. Observe, also, the strong emphasis on the need for continuing the project through its third, and final, year.

This is a report to the ABC Foundation covering the first two years of an experimental three-year Remedial Education Program conducted by XYZ Agency. The Foundation generously helped to assure continuation of this program through its second year with a grant of $.............................

We submit this report as an indication of what has been accomplished, and, also, with the deep hope that the ABC Foundation will

50

favorably consider making a grant of $............................ to finance the program through its third — and final — experimental year.

Background

XYZ Agency began its Remedial Education Program in mid-February of 19...... as a result of its observations that an increasing proportion of the boys and girls seeking the agency's help not only lacked advanced working skills, but, far more seriously, lacked even basic reading, writing and arithmetic skills, without which they could not even hope to acquire the advanced ones. Further investigation — by informal and formal testing — established that the lack of these basic academic skills did not necessarily reflect a lack of intelligence or of inability to learn, but, rather, was a consequence of inadequate and ineffective education.

Thus, as a pilot effort, XYZ Agency undertook its Remedial Education Program with these unique elements: It was designed to serve as an arm of the total guidance process, with counselors referring clients for remedial education and remaining in close touch with them while they participate in this program. To facilitate the continuing nature of the relationship, the program was to be offered directly on XYZ Agency premises. Finally, unlike the mass educational setting to which most of the youngsters were accustomed previously, instruction was to be provided on a one-to-one basis, except in special circumstances where it might be useful to have certain work done in small groups.

Results

The results of the program at this point are encouraging. During the the two-year period, 226 boys and girls received a total of 3,202 remedial sessions. Forty-seven cases are active and current. Thirty-five of the 179 terminated cases were closed for such reasons as youngsters having appeared for an initial interview only, or for evaluation only — or, as was the case with four boys, because of induction into the armed forces.

Of the remaining 144 terminated cases, 84 boys and girls,. more than 58 per cent, showed decided gains ranging from "graduating" to advanced training, usually in governmental programs, through actually finding work. (It is useful to recall that many of these young people, when they entered the project, were already failing in school, and that others were so lacking in basic educational skills that they could not apply for, much less hold, a job.)

Statistics are of course important in judging the value of any project. Alone, however, they cannot communicate the human factor, the changed attitudes of the youngsters toward themselves and society as they begin to experience a degree of success. Let us cite these two brief case histories:

(Two case histories follow.)

The Final Year

During the past two years, we have learned much about the needs and aspirations of culturally deprived young men and women who participated in the Remedial Education Program. We have learned of ways in which the community has failed them, and of ways in which we can, in part, at least, repair the damage.

The third and final experimental year — the year for which we ask the support of the ABC Foundation — is critical. Quite apart from the many boys and girls who will be helped, we shall be able to complete a full evaluation of the results of the program. Because of its uniqueness, we believe our findings may prove valuable to vocational counselors, schools and other agencies throughout the country.

Thus, for the sake of the youngsters who will be helped — and for the sake of the still-to-be-realized potential of our Remedial Education Program — we earnestly ask that the ABC Foundation favorably consider this appeal.

(Budget page follows.)

Usually, when one uses the phrase, "Special Project," it refers to an activity related to, but somehow separated from, a given institution's operational program. Many agencies, of course, approach foundations on this basis.

A few particularly alert organizations have gone one step further. Rather than ask for funds to undertake this or that project, they have asked for funds required *to raise* the funds for a variety of activities. In short, they have asked for seed money grants. This phrase falls pleasantly on the ears of most foundation executives, since it presumes that the grant seeker won't be around next year to ask for still another grant.

Following is a proposal prepared by a neighborhood center as it approached its 25th anniversary. The object: to secure a grant to enable it to conduct a 25th Anniversary Fund Raising Campaign.

As you read this proposal, note, among other points,

- that the neighborhood center indicates its faith in the project by assuming some of the cost of undertaking it. This also gives the foundation the assurance that, to an extent, anyway, the risk will be shared.

52

- that a specific financial goal is established, with the elements making up that goal fully spelled out. It is as important to indicate objectives, and how you expect to attain them, in this kind of presentation, as it is in a research project or in any other kind of special project.
- that the neighborhood center expects, if this "seed money" grant is made, to become self-sufficient and not to have to turn to the foundation for further support.

Beginning with 19....., the XYZ Neighborhood Center will celebrate its 25th anniversary. This represents more than an important milestone in our service to the upper Harlem community. It may mark the period in which the Center can, once and for all, put itself on a firm financial footing, able to meet the needs of its people in the most significant sense.

It is in this context that we ask ABC Foundation to consider making a grant of $35,500 to enable the XYZ Neighborhood Center to conduct a 25th anniversary fund raising and public relations campaign designed to establish a capital reserve of $350,000.

The total budget required for the campaign, which would commence October 1, 19..... and continue through the end of December, 19..... is $...................... Our financial resources already are severely limited. We believe, however, that prospects of success are exceptionally bright and our Board has pledged $10,000 toward the overall budget. For the remainder, we appeal to the ABC Foundation. The stability and growth of our agency — and, more important, the stability and growth of our community — are seriously involved.

OBJECTIVES

Our general objectives in establishing the 25th Anniversary Fund are:

1) to wipe out an accumulated operating deficit of $47,200.
2) to ensure the stability of the agency in its program of ongoing services.
3) to provide flexibility whereby XYZ may directly institute emergency programs in time of erupting stress. Our open air festivals, for example, tended to alleviate racial tensions during the summer of 19..... and helped to dissipate the simmering unrest which could easily have triggered riots.
4) to win understanding and support from a growing group of volunteers and contributors to the end that annual contributions will be increased in number and in amounts to keep pace with expanding budgets.

THE COMMUNITY

More than 170,000 people, mostly Negroes, Italians and Puerto Ricans, are concentrated in the 1½ square mile area that makes up the community. They must contend wtih problems of overcrowding, a juvenile delinquency rate that is among the highest in the city, racial tensions, and an all-pervasive poverty.

These people exist at a family income level which is substantially the lowest in the borough. Of those in the labor force, only 16 per cent have ever held a job for as long as a six-month period. More than 60 per cent of the young are school dropouts.

XYZ has constantly expanded the scope of its services in an effort to open up new avenues both of self-support and self-fulfillment for the community. Today, these services range from child care and mental hygiene for pre-schoolers to remedial reading for teenagers; from vocational training for young people to high school completion courses for mothers; from job placement for grandparents to street festivals for all our residents. As families have learned to use the Center and benefit from its resources, more and more of them turn to us for assistance — and for more and more varied forms of assistance. While we struggle to meet these ever-growing demands of a neighborhood in transition, we are confronted with an economy in which costs for providing *existing* services are constantly spiraling.

THE 25th ANNIVERSARY CAMPAIGN

Organization

The Board of Trustees will spearhead the campaign organization. For its chairman it will choose an influential and acknowledged civic leader with close ties to prospective donors and volunteers and to our people. He will be assisted by a steering committee, charged with the day-to-day decisions on campaign policies. This group will meet frequently with a professional campaign consultant and work closely with him.

Early in the campaign, the steering committee will enlist as Honorary Sponsors approximately 40 leaders from business, education, the arts and civic life to endorse the 25th Anniversary Fund and to focus the attention of the city at large on XYZ. Included also on the sponsoring committee will be outstanding representatives of the ethnic groups of upper Harlem and XYZ alumni who have established themselves as productive citizens.

The core of the fund raising campaign will be the volunteer committee functioning in the five distinct areas which our research and preliminary testing indicate hold the greatest potentials for success. These volunteer committees will be set up as follows:

Foundation Grants Committee — Amount to be raised: $180,000

At no time has XYZ possessed the financial resources to undertake a sustained effort to develop support from foundations. We have been unable to communicate with them as frequently as we should, nor have we been able to bring to their attention — effectively and dramatically — the expanding needs of the upper Harlem community, and the role XYZ seeks to play in meeting these needs. In light of this, it is of considerable importance to note that, over the past ten years, some 45 foundations have made grants to XYZ ranging from $200 to $25,000.

We mention this, first of all, to indicate the likelihood of success of a day-by-day foundations campaign. It is, however, equally important to note that many of these foundations — 25 — are not current contributors to XYZ.

Here, surely, in the context of our 25th Anniversary campaign, is a unique opportunity to re-establish relationships with these foundations, with a view to developing support for our Anniversary Fund.

Two further elements enhance our chances of success in the foundation field. They are:

- The wide range of foundations which XYZ can logically approach. Specifically, the quite large number of foundations concerned with youth and family welfare, with mental health, with the arts, with education, with inter-group relations, with vocational development, and with — broadly speaking — social welfare, can all find within XYZ's activities an area that falls within their sphere of interest.
- The one-time nature of the grant. Foundations, needless to say, are loath to make grants which may impose upon them an obligation for continual support of a given agency. Here, they are being asked to make a grant this once, and will consequently be free for other commitments in future years.

Implementing activities in the foundation field will be a committee including social welfare authorities who are well equipped to state the case for XYZ, Board members who may have access to foundation officials, and the Executive Director, who administers the program, and can offer detailed information on its operation.

Business and Corporate Gifts Committee — Amount to be raised: $45,000

A prominent business executive who is associated with XYZ either as a Board member, a donor, or a former or current area resident, will act as chairman of this committee. Aided by 15 to 20 leaders in commerce who are themselves in a position to approach successfully industrial organizations and their executives, he will explain and dramatize the special relationship of the business community to upper Harlem.

For business has — and knows it has — a self-interest at stake in the residents of upper Harlem. These people, many of whom have been unemployed for long periods of time, and are, therefore, a drain on the community economy and, on occasion, a threat to its peace and stability, can be aided so that they may become productive citizens, with a resultant gain not only to themselves, but to the city and its business community.

Special Gifts Committee — Amount to be raised: $65,000

XYZ already has a dedicated number of individuals who annually contribute to our program. Many of them, properly approached, will wish to mark the 25th Anniversary with commemorative gifts substantially increased in size. Many of them, too, will wish to serve as committee members and invite their own friends to help reach the goal.

Volunteers will be provided with lists drawn from regular contributors, lapsed donors and prospective givers. Records will be culled for former area residents, leaders of upper Harlem's ethnic groups, successful alumni and civic minded individuals and philanthropists with known interests in the problems which confront our people.

These prospective contributors will be invited to visit our Center and witness our program in operation. In some instances, they will be greeted by social workers who will explain the services and detail the results. In other instances, prospective donors may talk with our clients and discover directly the meaning of XYZ and its impact on those it serves. It is our expectation that financial assistance will follow and will be substantially greater in amount as a result of these personal visits.

Labor Unions Gifts Committee — Amount to be raised: $35,000

It is our plan to ask those labor leaders who are already our friends to be the nucleus of a Labor Unions Gifts Committee. They are currently few in number, but we are confident that these few will assist us and easily interest fellow leaders.

Key labor unions such as the International Ladies Garment Workers Union, the Brotherhood of Sleeping Car Porters and the Millinery Workers Union draw their membership from our community; they have demonstrated a keen interest in the welfare of their membership and they have, in addition, substantial health and welfare funds from which they contribute to community endeavors.

We expect that once we are in a position to acquaint them with our work — often through neighborhood people they know as their own — the labor unions will respond generously.

Special Projects Committee — Amount to be raised: $25,000

The Special Projects Committee will plan and organize two events such as a Chinese Auction and a theater party for those who wish to contribute to the 25th Anniversary Fund and can do so only on a relatively minor scale.

Those whom we serve will wish to help us mark the 25th Anniversary. That they may have a share in giving as well as in receiving, we will conduct a Chinese Auction, running perhaps for three nights. The sums involved will range from 25 cents to $3.00, so that no person, limited as he may be financially, will be deterred in his attempts to share in our fund raising efforts.

There are also young adults of limited income, outside the community, who have an interest in civic life and who will wish to make some contributions. They will be invited through their young friends, serving as volunteers, to participate in the theater party. This initial event will act as an introduction to XYZ.

The funds to be raised by these functions are of immediate importance; but we anticipate that the pattern of giving which will be initiated during the campaign will continue in succeeding years and that the gifts will increase as these donors find their incomes rising.

Public Relations Program

The public relations program will focus on volunteers, prospective donors and the public at large.

For volunteers and prospective donors, printed materials will include a statement of purpose, a 25th Anniversary brochure, letters of appeal, pledge cards, acknowledgments, invitations, special presentations and campaign bulletins.

News and general feature releases, to be distributed to the mass media, will center on the activities of the 25th Anniversary Fund as well as on the program of XYZ. In this way, the volunteers and the donors will receive additional recognition for their contributions while the image of XYZ is being impressed upon the public mind.

The 25th Anniversary year offers a solid news peg on which to hang feature stories on XYZ, for the Center has within its services a lode of untouched, fresh subject matter which will find ready acceptance by editors. For example, its Women's Employment Committee, through which Harlem housewives are effectively taking themselves out of domestic service and into offices and department stores, has never been publicized. Such a story can highlight the pioneering services of XYZ and the promise of those it serves. Interviews with the Executive Director and President of the Board of Trustees can be used to describe the growth of the agency; picture stories of outdoor entertainments can highlight the close relationship between XYZ and the community.

These are but a few of the newsworthy stories which will substantiate the appeals of volunteers to donors while they inform the public at large.

SUMMARY

The ABC Foundation has distinguished itself by its venturesomeness, by its willingness to provide seed money for a given project when the project offers a reasonable hope of leading to long-term benefits of a highly significant nature.

The fund raising and public relations program we have described is such a project. In a sense, the 25th Anniversary campaign represents the last good chance for XYZ to secure the resources required to achieve its guiding purposes: to better the lives of the residents of upper Harlem, and, in so doing, to better the lives of all who live and work in our city.

To these ends, we respectfully request the support of the ABC Foundation.

(Budget page follows)

Writing the Building Proposal

A noted authority on advertising whose name escapes us once said, "The secret of success in advertising is that you don't sell the steak, you sell the sizzle."

So it is with building presentations. For whatever else a building may be, it is also an inert mass of brick and concrete and mortar and wood and lots of other things that don't live. Your job is to make your building live . . . by stressing its function, by spelling out why the services it will make possible are so special and necessary.

In essence, then, in one way or another, you will nearly always be talking about people. If it is a hospital you want built, you will talk about people who need care and treatment to get well; if a day care center, about working mothers who must have a place where their children will be safe and happy; if a college, about the process of learning that will take place in the building and the advancement of knowledge that will result.

In short, you will find in a well written building proposal that far more time will be spent in talking about the program than in talking about the building.

Let's now analyze this first example from a neighborhood school for the arts on the west coast. Earlier, you will recall, we mentioned that when you have a longish presentation, it is frequently a good idea to reduce its essence to one summary page. Once having done this, the summary page becomes both an opportunity and a danger. If it is compellingly written, it may go a long way in convincing a given foundation official of the wisdom of making a grant; it surely will induce him to read the full proposal. On the other hand, if the summary page communicates little or no excitement, chances are that the reading of the proposal will end right there:

59

SUMMARY

XYZ Agency is planning to build, in the heart of .... the nation's first community arts workshop designed specifically for a predominantly disadvantaged, multicultural population. Its objective is to offer, under one roof, a variety of arts programs of high quality that will have relevance to the diverse neighborhood groups: Chicano, black, white middle-class, and Chinese.

To be known as the Community Workshop for the Performing Arts, the new building will house XYZ's long-established and highly regarded programs, molded to the needs of today's urban slum.

When it begins to function, the Workshop will accomplish several large designs simultaneously:

- It will guarantee that the high excellence that has characterized XYZ's instruction in music, dance, drama, and the fine arts will continue in appropriate surroundings;

- It will, we believe, bring a new sense of pride and dignity to .... that will be a powerful force in sustaining the neighborhood as well as in providing a continuity into the future for its rich cultural heritage;

- And it will bring together, in one setting, perhaps the most diverse ethnic, cultural and economic groups that exist in this country. As it develops the best that is in these people by the way of artistic expression, we believe it will also deepen their understanding, not only of themselves, but of each other.

The Community Workshop for the Performing Arts will be located on .... Street. The projected cost of equipping and building the new structure is $1.5 million. At this point, XYZ has raised $500,-000, of which members of its Board and their families have given over $300,000. With this significant progress, and with an active committee of civic minded men and women pursuing additional sources of help for large grants, XYZ Agency expects to begin construction by the fall of this year.

XYZ programs, in general, have sought to knit this varied, sometimes torn, sometimes violent community into a more harmonious whole. We are convinced that the Community Workshop for the Performing Arts

60

will play a major role in this effort in the years to come. By making art an integral part of people's lives, this new resource will not only contribute to the advancement of the arts themselves, but to the building of a healthier, more unified city.

Towards these objectives, we submit the enclosed proposal with a request for a grant of $100,000 from the ABC Foundation.

One of the more significant points to be noted with regard to the preceding summary page is that it has been written so as to appeal to the interests of a wide range of foundations. Obviously, foundations that prefer to give for building purposes (of which there are a fair number) will have no trouble, at least as far as policy is concerned, in making a grant for the building. Nor will a foundation interested in cultural matters. This applies also to foundations whose first interest may be education. And going beyond this, foundations whose interests may be as far afield as inter-racial matters or in the problems of minority people also have been given a reason for giving. Even foundations whose sole concern may be with civic betterment can find a reason why they shoulld give (Later in this section you will see how this same proposal might be refined to be directed specifically at a certain kind of foundation.)

Note also certain other points in the Summary:

- The uniqueness of the building's purpose is made clear. It will be "the nation's first community arts workshop designed specifically for a predominately disadvantaged, multicultural population."

- The financial commitment of the Board—an important consideration with foundations—is spelled out. Members and their families have given over $300,000.

- A sense of on-goingness—of a building that really will rise—is communicated by the fact that the agency "expects fo begin construction by the fall of this year."

- And, finally, a specified amount—$100,000—is requested. XYZ Agency has done its homework and—based on the pattern of giving by the foundation—knows that this is at least a feasible amount.

The formal proposal itself follows. Since both the summary and the proposal are intended to stand as self-contained units, there is a slight duplication of language. Note, again how heavily the proposal is oriented toward program, although there is also a section on the specific architecture of the building.

This is a request to the ABC Foundation from XYZ Agency for a grant of $100,000 towards a Community Workshop for the Performing Arts that will bring together in one complex all of XYZ's distinguished schools and programs in the arts. This will include: the Music School; the School of Dance and Drama; the Pottery and Art School; the Film and Photography Workshops; and a special neighborhood arts program —all directed toward engaging the broadest possible participation from a predominantly disadvantaged population.

The unique aspect of this multiple arts resource, is that it will serve a community of diverse cultural and economic levels and people of all age groups. Its objective is to serve the total community—the severely disadvantaged as well as the advantaged, the young as well as the elderly, while maintaining the high standards of excellence that have been the hallmark of XYZ arts programs.

The Projected cost of building and equipping the new structure is $1.5 million. XYZ Board members and their families have themselves already contributed, or pledged, an amount in excess of $300,000.

(A section on the background of XYZ Agency and its development as a leading school for the arts appears here.)

The Neighborhood. The population served by XYZ Agency today, is made up of diverse cultural and economic groups. Low-income public housing projects and old law tenements provide housing for families of marginal incomes and the very poor; middle-income cooperatives have brought to the neighborhood a white middle class population. According to demographic projections, the population majority is, and continues to be, black, with a Mexican-American minority and a still smaller minority of Chinese families. XYZ's approach to the goal of integrating these groups is double-pronged: through building and program. We are here concerned with the building that will house a program that is already in progress.

The new building will occupy the block on .... Street. This is in the designated area of an urban renewal program known as ....

....

The Community Workshop for the Performing Arts will provide an additional dimension in the renewed area. Together with better homes, the residents will have in their midst a resource that will permit the widest possible participation in the arts by all segments of the community.

ROLE OF THE COMMUNITY WORKSHOP FOR THE PERFORMING ARTS

Because the arts programs at XYZ Agency involve people of many ethnic and economic groups, the XYZ has a unique opportunity to create a dramatic, new type of cultural institution; one that can serve today's urban neighborhood with programs that will have significance and excitement to people as diverse as the graduate of an ivy league college and the ghetto youth with a third-grade reading level. It differs from traditional art centers in that its objective is not to impose art on a community but to draw art from it, and to find art wherever it exists. Some of the unusual features of the new Community Workshop will be:

1. It will emphasize participation rather than observation.

2. Its users will have a part in planning and operating the program.

3. It will be family-oriented, having family memberships, and offering activities for elderly people, adults, young adults, teenagers and pre-schoolers. This aspect is of particular pertinence since many of the residents are of limited mobility and their world very often consists of the three or four blocks around their homes.

4. The new building will add beauty and dignity to a community that is in the process of becoming improved physically through the elimination of decaying slums. It will reflect in its design the philosophy of its purpose; to be an open door to the arts for all who enter. The program that will emanate from it will, in turn, offer dignity and self esteem to its participants, many of whom have too long been cut off from avenues of advancement by roadblocks which poverty has placed in their way.

THE ARTS AT XYZ AGENCY

XYZ Agency, since its founding in 1911 has always placed strong emphasis on the arts.

(A description of each of the arts schools at XYZ Agency appears here).

Out of the Civil Rights Movement and the search for social justice by minority groups has come a heightened interest among blacks and Chicanos in their cultural heritage. XYZ Agency has been quick to respond to this and to provide these groups with arts activities which grow out of their life experiences. Dance, drama, music, film, sculpture and painting are all means through which the black and Mexican-American people are in touch with their own background and communicate their particular points of view.

Teachers of the educationally disadvantaged in the schools have often been unsuccessful on helping these young people develop skills in communication. Yet, XYZ has found that many of the same children who have done poorly in school are able to communicate ideas vividly and present significant points of view about themselves and the world around them through the use of motion pictures and still photography. Films made by young people at XYZ have been featured on nationwide television, and one film was awarded a prize at the city-wide film festival.

XYZ is also offering programs in Spanish music and has organized a successful steel drum band. It also provides facilities and opportunities for various teenage rock and Latin American groups to make music. Similarly classes in pottery, painting, batik and tie dye printing of fabrics, sewing and dress designing, woodcraft and photography are offered to adults and elderly residents as well as to children. Here, the emphasis is on the act of creative self expression.

Whereas these activities now take place in many locations and centers operated by XYZ, they will be concentrated in the Community Workshop for the Performing Arts along with the more formal programs once the new building becomes a reality.

THE COMMUNITY WORKSHOP FOR THE PERFORMING ARTS —ITS ARCHITECTURE

At XYZ Agency, we have always placed greater emphasis on program than on bricks and mortar and, therefore, we view this new structure, not as just another cultural center, but as an instrument that will extend and deepen our entire concept of the arts as a basic human right.

A young and able architect, Mr. .... , of the firm, ... , has designed an economical structure which responds to XYZ's

64

need for flexibility, includes the facilities most wanted by the residents of the community, and will be an architecturally attractive addition to the neighborhood.

The new building will occupy a lot area of 10,500 square feet, of approximately 100x100. It will be built of reinforced concrete with exterior walls of brick, and it will be fully air conditioned.

Unlike traditional structures, rather than standard size stories, the center will be built on several levels, with the studios, workshops and classrooms unwinding in tier-like fashion around a semicircular corridor until they have reached the height of approximately a two story building. Its facilities therefore, will be found on a garden level (partially below ground); on the street level; on the terrace level (balcony or deck); and on the third level (second floor).

Some of the unusual features of the new workshop are described below.

(Specific architectural elements appear here).

CONCLUSION

The Community Workshop for the Performing Arts will be the gathering of the poor and the not-so-poor, of newcomers and long-time residents, of the very young and of the elderly, of artists and students. It will be the means through which these varied and diverse neighborhood groups can participate in the use of the arts as a means of communication and creative self expression. Like other XYZ experimental programs, the Workshop will attract young, gifted enthusiastic instructors who want to be part of a developing program. By making art an integral part of the people's lives, this new resource will not only contribute to the advancement of the arts, themselves, but to the building of a healthier and more unified city.

In submitting this proposal, XYZ Agency most earnestly hopes that the Trustees of the ABC Foundation will share its commitment to this program. To this end, we, respectfully ask your support.

Chapter I is concerned with getting foundation appointments. How important this is in the process of securing grants is illustrated in the following proposal which deals with precisely the same subject as the preceeding one. It is—obviously—much shorter and takes the form of a letter. But—much more important—note that concepts in Points 2 and 3 do not appear at all in the earlier presentation. Without question, information communicated at the foundation meeting helped shape the content of the proposal.

Dear Mr. .... :

I remain appreciative of your courtesy in meeting with me to discuss the proposed Community Workshop of the Performing Arts. As you suggested, I am now submitting a formal proposal requesting the support of the ABC Foundation.

Some vital statistics first: The cost of the new building will be $1.5 million. Eighteen months of intensive fund raising has brought us to the verge of being able to go ahead with the building. We have, thus far, raised $1.3 million, of which our Board contributed over $400,000. It is my hope that the ABC Foundation will favorably consider making a grant of $25,000, thus bringing us significantly closer to the amount required for construction.

There are many compelling reasons which we could cite as justification for a grant from the ABC Foundation, but in the interests of brevity I shall limit myself to only three:

1. *The Community Workshop as an Educational Facility.* When constructed, the new building will guarantee that the high excellence th has characterized XYZ Agency instruction in the arts will continue in appropriate surroundings. It will bring together in one setting the XYZ Music School, the School of Dance and Drama, the Art and Pottery School, the Neighborhood Arts Program, and the Film and Photography Workshop. All of these activities presently are operating at capacity enrollment in wholly inadequate space, widely dispersed from each other.

2. *The Community Workshop as a National Institution.* The Community Workshop represents at one and the same time a dual institution. It will be, obviously, a vital neighborhood resource, serving its community and, indeed residents from every part of the city, as well as a fair number outside of it.

Beyond this, the Workshop will serve as national laboratory for creative self-expression by people of the inner city. It will be the first arts center designed for a predominantly disadvantaged, multi-culture population. And as such, we believe its impact will be nationwide in the kind of courses it offers, as well as in the techniques that it develops.

3. *The Community Workshop as a Seed Money Investment.* XYZ Agency draws its support for its programs, including those in the arts, from a nationwide network of friends. With this support, we are able to carry out our programs, but it is not enough to bring into existence the Community Workshop for the Performing Arts. A one-time grant from the ABC Foundation will, in effect, help create the platform from which these programs will spring for many, many years.

I have tried to be brief. But, if you like, there is still lots of information we can give you—the actual building plans, the backgrond of each of our schools, the names of the foundations which have already contributed significantly toward the Workshop, as well as anything else you might want to know. If you—or any Trustees of the Foundation—could find the time to visit us, I would be delighted to guide you through our programs, as well as have you inspect the site of the Community Workshop.

Again, let me say how pleasant it was to meet you. We shall all look forward to your response.

Sincerely,

Obtaining a new building doesn't always mean building it. It can, as is the case with the example that follows, mean purchasing it. That fact doesn't really alter anything. You are still selling the "sizzle". Note, however, the effective use of contrasts "1,800 square feet served a staff of 16—now it must serve 44" or "our population is expected to grow from today's 300,000 to nearly half a million". Note also that foundations are expected to put up no more than one-third of the funds required.

Dear Mr. .... :

I am writing to ask the ABC Foundation to make a one-time contribution toward the cost of new headquarters building for XYZ Agency, which will enable us to improve our effectiveness vastly in rendering full home health services to .... 's exploding population.

67

Through contributions and pledges by our board of directors, mostly men and women of moderate means, we are already more than one-third of the way toward our goal of $100,000.

More space is urgently needed. The 1,800 square feet that served a staff of sixteen in 19.... cannot begin to accommodate our present 44-member staff.

In the past thirty years, ... 's population doubled. To meet its needs, we added four new programs—physical therapy, psychiatric nursing, nutrition and a home health aide service—and expanded our old ones. Stimulated by the new .... Freeway. Our population is expected to grow from today's 300,000 to nearly half-a-million by 1980. We must grow with it.

(Description of physical limitations appears here).

The most painful aspect of all is the necessity of turning away people who need our help. We must hire five additional visiting nurses and two more physical therapists to meet the demand, but we have absolutely no further space.

Patients who require their services must do without until we have it.

The $100,000 building we have contracted to buy on the strength of our board's support is centrally located, will meet present needs without alterations and will allow room for growth. We must buy because our limited reserves will not safely support the addition of high rental fees to our current operating deficit. We felt also that our friends and supporters would more willingly contribute to a one-time campaign to purchase a building.

Along with the one-third pledged by our board, we anticipate an additional third in pledges and contributions by local industries. We must turn to foundations for the remaining third.

To help us meet the health challenges we face now and those that will rise out of .... 's future growth I ask that The ABC Foundation favorably consider making a one-time grant of $5,000 toward the remaining balance of our building campaign.

I have enclosed a copy of our current annual report and, if you wish any further information, I will be delighted to supply it.

Sincerely,

We noted earlier the desirability of keeping your proposal brief and uncluttered, while presenting your supporting material in the form of appendices. Here is an example of such a proposal, a request from a community center for a grant of a considerable amount of money to renovate completely its summer camp for underprivileged children.

Among other points, note the following:

- The amount requested, $205,600, is rather too much to expect from one foundation for this purpose — hence the phrase in the opening paragraph, "or a portion of this amount."
- The community center, in effect, guarantees that it will not be coming back for operating or maintenance funds.
- The new facilities will permit a greatly expanded program.

This is a request to the ABC Foundation from XYZ Community Center for a grant of $205,600, or a portion of this amount, to finance the complete renovation of our day camp facilities at Spring Valley, New York. Of the total amount, $98,600 will be utilized to repair and convert 27 old buildings formerly used for resident campers; $107,000 will be used for the construction of recreational facilities.

This grant will provide — year after year — day camp facilities for a total program for 1,050 underprivileged girls and boys now on our long waiting lists. They will come to Spring Valley Camp in groups of 350 for each of our three encampments.

XYZ Community Center has conducted a day camp program, limited in size and in scope, on an experimental basis for the past four years. On the basis of this successful experiment and the ever-increasing demands for services, we are prepared to launch an expanded day camp program.

With the proposed conversion and construction, these deprived youngsters will be offered a complete outdoor program of recreational, educational and civic activities under specially trained adult supervision. For many youngsters, these camp experiences will provide not only a summer vacation but direction and guidance for the future.

We are assured of the operating funds with which to support an on-going program for the 1,050 youngsters, from three to twelve years old. Moreover, we can underwrite the maintenance costs required to keep the facilities, once they are repaired, in prime condition for many years of use.

But the existing physical facilities are unsafe and hazardous. They cannot be used in their present condition, and we cannot undertake a permanent program until the buildings have been repaired. These shelters are essential. They serve as the core around which the entire day camp program revolves. Each age group assembles in its own shelter when its members arrive by bus for the day's activities. Here, the youngsters have protection against cold and rain, and space for rest periods and indoor play. They have here, too, facilities for changing in and out of bathing suits and storage areas for lunches, extra sweaters and accumulations of their camp treasures. Showers, toilets and washbasins are a necessity for each group. Group recreational supplies are housed in these buildings.

A playground for each of the five age groups is essential for a fully rounded program. Each play area will be built and equipped to fulfill the recreational needs and meet the physical requirements of one age group. In addition, we plan to dredge and enlarge an existing reservoir for boating and fishing for all. The estimated costs for these facilities are $50,000.

Our day camp youngsters have been sharing the swimming pool built for our resident campers. It is small, but 25 feet wide by 75 feet long, and cannot accommodate the numbers who wish to use it. During the past summer, time allotted to both resident and day camp groups was necessarily held to 35 minutes. These periods were totally inadequate, hurried and unsatisfying. The children lacked the time for learning to swim, for improving their skills at the sport and even for enjoying the water. Additional youngsters in such numbers cannot be added to the already crowded schedule. A new pool at a cost of $52,000 will free the old one for the resident campers and offer to the day campers a major activity for physical development and for vacation fun and relaxation.

It is for the construction of these recreational facilities and for the repair of our basic shelters that we appeal to the ABC Foundation.

We are attaching schematics of the new construction at camp, together with budgets, as well as some particular background information on XYZ Community Center.

Here is another example of a request for building funds. When you have done your homework well, that is, when you have made certain that you are approaching the right foundation, your letter may almost write itself.

As you will note, in this letter from an organization helping handicapped children, the writing is very simple and to the point.

Dear ....:

Let me thank you, first of all, for your prompt reply to my letter requesting a meeting with Mr. ....

We do, indeed, feel that the project we have in mind is one in which the ABC Foundation will be deeply interested. Quite simply, we are applying for a grant of $..................... to enable us to make repairs essential to keeping in operation a dormitory for handicapped boys at ....New York.

Let us give you this brief background:

In 19...., XYZ Agency established one of the first summer camps for handicapped children in the United States. A pioneering camp at that time, it remains one now, playing an integral role in helping handicapped children make a satisfactory adjustment to normal community life. The camp is operated on a nonsectarian, interracial basis, with the preponderance of the children coming from families on welfare.

In 19..... the agency raised sufficient funds to build a new boys' dormitory. Since that time, the dormitory has served its children well. During the summer it accommodates twenty-eight boys, each of whom received a full month's vacation. Last year, just before vacation season, it was discovered that the floor was rotting away. In making spot emergency repairs, it was also discovered that the beams beneath the floor had deteriorated to the point that, in the words of the contractor, "they have the consistency of sand." By summer 19....., the floor will be totally unsafe, and, hence, the dormitory will be unusable.

The cost of installing a new floor is $....................., and we have enclosed the estimate of ...., a licensed building and contracting firm.

This, to us, is a staggering sum. As you will note from the enclosed financial statement, we concluded the 19..... fiscal year with a deficit of $..................... . Our deficit for 19..... may approach $..................... .

Quite frankly, we have no resource to turn to other than the ABC Foundation. Without your help it may be necessary for us to have to deprive twenty-eight physically handicapped boys of what to them is more than just a summer's vacation, but rather a means of achieving the potential that lies within them.

With all the earnestness and sincerity we possess, we appeal for your favorable consideration.

Very truly yours,

Letters Of Renewal

The most important thing to remember in asking a foundation to renew an annual grant is that, to the extent possible, it appear that your letter could not have been prepared for anyone else. This is, of course, true of all appeal letters. With foundations, however, you usually will have files of correspondence to draw upon. Here, for example, is the way a college began a renewal letter to several foundations from which it had been receiving grants for a period of 15 to 20 years.

Dear ....:

It is interesting — and rather moving — to note that most of the young men and women attending XYZ College were playing with erector sets and dolls when the ABC Foundation made its first grant to the college. It would be hard to estimate how many thousands of students secured a better education at this college as a result of your generosity over the years.

Here, again, is the same college writing to a foundation which had made its first grant a year earlier.

Dear ....:

In reading over our correspondence of the previous year, I was struck by a phrase in which you expressed your enthusiasm for the way our small library in the Union Building functioned.

There have been a number of developments with regard to the library, and I would like to tell you about them . . .

Sometimes it is useful, when approaching a foundation for renewal of its grant, not only to include news of significant developments, but, also, to restate the basic philosophy of your organization.

Here is how an agency concerned with interracial relationships did so:

Dear .... :

Last year at this season, the ABC Foundation made a generous grant of $............... toward the work of XYZ Agency. I think you known how grateful we were — and are.

In view of your thoughtful support, I believe you will find particularly interesting the enclosed brief report on a new program recently undertaken by XYZ Agency — the .... Educational Project. We have great hopes for this project and, I believe, you may find the report to be a moving, perhaps inspiring, document.

This new project is one of a number that XYZ Agency has recently introduced. In a time of deep unrest, we have felt that we must not hold back in offering the black community responsible programs of substance and meaning with regard to employment, housing, equal opportunity and leadership development.

It is no secret that the movement for Negro rights stands at a crossroads, and that the direction it takes will affect not Negroes alone, but the nation as a whole. We believe firmly that the direction must be one of increasing partnership between men of good will, between black and white.

Thus, as we work more and more intensively to meet the ghetto problems of despair, of frustration, and of deep rooted bitterness, we need more than ever before the support of all of our old friends.

May I be bold enough to ask that the ABC Foundation consider increasing its grant to $...............? Such a grant will do much to enable us to expand our programs at a time in which the need for them has never been greater.

Needless to say, I would be more than happy to provide whatever additional information you might require.

Sincerely,

Note two more things about the previous letter. It establishes immediately that the grant is due for renewal at that particular time. (Usually, letters of this kind should go into the mails six to eight weeks earlier than the date at which the gift arrived the previous year.)

The letter also asks that the grant be increased. Unless there are compelling reasons for not doing so, this should be your practice, too. Obviously, you have to build a case for an increase, or, to use a phrase that should be familiar, a "special circumstance." (Re-read the section on general purpose letters.)

Depending on the situation, it may or may not be useful to specify the amount of the increase, as the previous letter did. Asking for an increase, though, whether the amount is specified or not, is one good way of helping to assure that you will not end up by getting less than before.

This is how an organization working with physically handicapped children presented its case for an increase in its grant.

Dear ....:

I am writing, first of all, to say how very much we appreciate the grant of $........................ made last year at this time by the ABC Foundation to XYZ Agency, and, also, to express the hope that the Foundation will consider a substantial increase in the grant for this year. I have made this request for two reasons.

The first is that XYZ has developed important new services which can be put into full operation only with increased support. The second is that there has been an almost spectacular increase in the number of families turning to XYZ for help.

(The remainder of the letter goes on to document the previous paragraph.)

Sincerely,

At this point, it should be obvious that one of the keys to successfully renewing grants is to make your letters sound like something more than just a request for renewal of a grant. Frequently, as in the previous examples, this is done by presenting new information or by indicating special program needs, etc. Occasionally, it is desirable not only to do these things, but also to alter the format you have been utilizing. Again, this communicates a sense of something more than routine, of something important. The first paragraph of the following letter illustrates this point.

Dear Mr.   :

This year, rather than the usual letter, we are submitting a formal presentation in which we ask you to double your annual grant to XYZ Hospital. The presentation offers striking evidence of how urgently needed by our community are the services of the Hospital; and how these needs are likely to grow in the years ahead.

Next to a currently giving foundation, the foundation most likely to make a grant to your organization is the one that used to give but stopped. Obviously, then, you should spend a good deal of time with your file of lapsed foundations, seeking some means of restoring the gift. It will undoubtedly be helpful if a friendly relationship should exist between a member of your board and a foundation trustee. But, even without this, you should persist.

Your approach may be as simple, brief and straightforward as that embodied in the letter from an interracial organization that follows immediately. Or you can try a broader, more detailed approach, as indicated by the second letter, from a community center.

Dear   :

I am writing to ask the ABC Foundation to restore the generous grant of $ which it made to XYZ Agency in 19 .

The ABC Foundation already knows us, and I shall not attempt here to detail the many pioneering ways in which this agency has helped Negroes and Puerto Ricans to achieve a fuller measure of equality in education, employment and housing. I would only say that XYZ Agency now stands at a critical point in maintaining and expanding its services. We need, as never before, the support of all our old friends.

Most earnestly, I hope you will favorably consider this request.

If there is any additional information you might wish, I would be delighted to provide it.

Sincerely,

P. S.   Our most recent Annual Report is enclosed.

Dear ....:

I enclose the 19..... Annual Report of XYZ Community Center with a mixture of pride and hope — pride in some rather remarkable accomplishments for an agency as small as ours — and hope that the ABC Foundation, in weighing these accomplishments and the goals we have set for ourselves, will favorably consider restoring its support to XYZ Community Center.

The great dream of our Center — establishment of XYZ Prep School — became a reality. Now, for the first time in its history, Harlem has its own college preparatory school — a gateway for kids from the ghetto to resume their education and continue into college. XYZ Prep begins operations in January. But, already, we have succeeded in enrolling more than 100 youths — dropouts, delinquents, kids from broken homes, and worse — into such institutions as ....

....

All told, over .... ghetto youngsters are currently participating in this project. Every one of them comes from a background of social and educational failure. Based on our previous experience, we are confident that the great majority will achieve academic secondary diplomas, and that a high proportion will go on to either junior college or to college. It is impossible to say how much this may mean to these youths, to their community and to this city.

I shall not dwell on still other breakthroughs which were made by XYZ Community Center. Briefly, however, we experienced the greatest one-year increase in our history in the demand for our day-to-day services. The number of young people enrolled in our programs rose over .... per cent, from .... to ....

Finally, our Employment Guidance Program placed scores of qualified Negroes and Puerto Ricans in good paying positions — positions which they had no chance of getting less than a few years ago, no matter how well qualified they were.

XYZ Community Center now stands at the threshold of making its most meaningful contribution, not only to its community, but to its city as a whole. The support given to us by the ABC Foundation helped bring us to that point. For whatever reason, the Foundation was unable to renew its grant of $............... in 19..... Most earnestly, I hope it will now do so.

Sincerely,

As a final point in our discussion regarding renewing grants, let us ask the question, when is a terminal grant not a terminal grant? The answer is that it need never be terminal, if you continue to persist. A vocational guidance agency, for example, had received a quite substantial grant, specified as "one-time", from a particular foundation. Over the next two years, however, the agency began exploring new areas of service, as well as undertaking certain special projects. It successfully approached the same foundation as before, and this is the covering letter it used:

Dear ....:

When the ABC Foundation so generously made a grant of $.................. to XYZ Agency in 19....., it did so with the stipulation that it be considered a one-time gift.

In view of a special situation that has developed at XYZ, I am taking the liberty of asking whether it might be possible to waive that stipulation.

Last year, we undertook a Vocational Guidance Project for former alcoholics. Begun as an experiment, this program has proved so constructive that we are most anxious to continue it for another year. We do not possess the funds to do so. Fortunately, however, we have secured over 50% of the required financing from two foundations.

I am submitting with this letter an application describing this project in some detail. It is my earnest hope that the ABC Foundation will recognize the special circumstances surrounding my request, as well as the need and value of the project, and favorably consider helping XYZ once again.

Sincerely,

Needless to say, any renewal of a grant should be promptly acknowledged. Your "Thank you" letter should not be effusive, nor need it be long. It should, of course, communicate a sense of warmth and appreciation, as do the two examples that follow:

Dear .... :

The ABC Foundation's generous contribution to XYZ Agency will be put to work in many ways for many young people having trouble finding their way into a difficult adult world.

Many thanks—from those who work to maintain XYZ services, and from those who benefit from those services.

Please convey our gratitude to the trustees of the Foundation.

Sincerely,

Dear .... :

Thank you very much for the ABC Foundation's increased gift to XYZ Hospital.

These are difficult days for voluntary agencies like ours. To make operating income keep pace with constantly increasing operating expenses is all but impossible. We are grateful to the ABC Foundation for helping us reduce the gap between the two.

Please convey our appreciation to the trustees of the Foundation.

Sincerely,

Conclusion

It is evident that no one can set down a series of rules and regulations which will guarantee that you will write a good foundation proposal. Obviously, some very crucial elements — your sense of logic, your sensitivity and your creativity — cannot be handed down to you.

However, by way of summary, and also to mention a few points which didn't find their way into the earlier pages, here are some general guidelines for writing successful foundation presentations.

- Presentations should be single spaced and typed on one side of the page only. They should never be mimeographed, nor should "fill-ins" be utilized.

- Presentations should be kept as brief as possible, usually no more than five pages (less, if you can), including neither the title page nor the budget page. Additional necessary materials should be included in the form of appendices.

- Letters requesting appointments must be kept brief, introducing no more than the essential information. If no response is received, you should follow up with a telephone call.

- Letters requesting general purpose grants should present a special circumstance justifying such a grant.

- A special project presentation should somehow be larger than itself; that is to say it should have a multiplying or rippling effect.

- When writing for renewal of a grant, ask for more than was previously given.

- In all foundation proposals, and particularly special project presentations, say the important things first. The basic purpose of the project should be stated within the first paragraph. Also, what it will cost. Your chances of getting a special project grant are better if you ask for the funds before starting the project rather than afterward.

- Foundations are happier when they feel you will not be coming back to them with repeated requests for grants. If your request is in the nature of a one-time grant, make a point of saying so.

- Foundations also like to see someone — in addition to themselves — providing the financing. If you have already secured partial funding for a given project, either from other foundations, from an individual, or perhaps out of your agency's own resources, make sure you mention this.

- You should be specific about the amount of money you require — either in a well itemized budget page in a special project presentation, or as a stated amount in a general purpose proposal. Your budget is a picture — in dollars and cents — of the total project. Don't make mistakes such as not allowing for normal increments if the project is intended to last more than one year.

- *It goes without saying that the foundation you are approaching has demonstrated an interest in your field.*